Henry Shaw's Victorian Landscapes

Henry Shaw's Victorian Landscapes

THE MISSOURI BOTANICAL GARDEN

AND TOWER GROVE PARK

Carol Grove

UNIVERSITY OF MASSACHUSETTS PRESS   AMHERST & BOSTON

IN ASSOCIATION WITH

LIBRARY OF AMERICAN LANDSCAPE HISTORY   AMHERST

Printed in China

LC 2005011749
ISBN 1-55849-508-8

Designed by Jonathan D. Lippincott

Set in Granjon, Eva Antiqua, and Kabel Demi

Printed and bound by C&C Offset Printing Co., Ltd.

Library of Congress Cataloging-in-Publication Data
Grove, Carol.
    Henry Shaw's Victorian landscapes : the Missouri Botanical Garden and Tower
Grove Park / Carol Grove.
       p. cm.
"In association with Library of American Landscape History, Amherst."
    Includes bibliographical references and index.
    ISBN 1-55849-508-8 (cloth : alk. paper)
 1. Shaw, Henry, 1800–1889. 2. Botanizers—Missouri—Saint Louis—Biography.
3. Missouri Botanical Garden—History. 4. Tower Grove Park (Saint Louis, Mo.)—
History. I. Title.
    QK31.S47G76 2006
    580.73778'66—dc22
                                                                        2005011749

British Library Cataloguing in Publication data are available.

Illustrations of Tower Grove Park unless otherwise credited
are courtesy of Tower Grove Park Archives.

All other illustrations unless otherwise credited
are courtesy of Missouri Botanical Garden Archives.

FRONTISPIECE: The grove and Tower Grove House. Photo by Carol Betsch.

Publication of this book was supported by a generous gift from
Jane and Joe Gleason in loving memory of Marion and Vernon Piper.

Contents

Preface

For many people, the prototypical nineteenth-century landscape is Olmstedian—calming and restorative, with tree-rimmed clearings, wooded rambles, and small lakes, features disposed in pictorial compositions that evoke idyllic countryside. This genre of landscape has been the subject of extended study, in LALH books and elsewhere, and, as a result, it is much better understood than it once was. But this, of course, was not the whole story.

Other sorts of landscapes were developed during these years, too, by individuals whose temperaments differed from that of Frederick Law Olmsted, and who were motivated by different goals. One such individual was the Englishman Henry Shaw (1800–1889), who wanted clarity, not mystery, order, not irregular incident, and plants for study, not repose. The present book by Carol Grove, an art historian who has specialized in the gardenesque in America, sheds welcome light on Shaw's purposes in designing two great landscapes in St. Louis, the Missouri Botanical Garden and Tower Grove Park.

Grove traces her hero—and he is surely a hero—from his birth in Sheffield, England, to his immigration to America at age eighteen, and then to his very successful business life in St. Louis.

Once he had made his fortune, the young bachelor began to travel, and over the course of these travels (to England, the Continent, Russia, and the Near East) he was inspired to bring back ideas to improve his adopted home, which was still something of a raw boomtown. During his second Grand Tour, Shaw was "bitten" by gardening, in particular, the English style then guiding his former countryman William Spencer Cavendish, the sixth duke of Devonshire.

Shaw began to imagine how he, too, could create a great garden. He liked to ride his horse over the undulating prairie on the outskirts of town, land that we would certainly describe as beautiful, if, indeed, any remnants of it were left. But, to Shaw, the prairie was a featureless canvas, and he planned to transform it with a remarkable display of plants, a garden of greater size and scope than nearly any other in the United States.

Shaw began planting his private garden about 1849, almost immediately after commissioning Tower Grove, his Italianate country villa. One senses, from the staggering numbers and varieties listed in his plant orders (still meticulously preserved) that the impetus for his public enterprise a few years later grew directly from the private endeavor. Simply put, once Shaw started, he could not stop. But while his personal garden was an enlightened amateur effort, his botanical garden was undertaken with advice from the highest authorities in the field, John Claudius Loudon, Sir Joseph Paxton, William Hooker, and, in this country, Asa Gray. He also relied heavily on George Engelmann, a medical doctor, serendipitously located in St. Louis, who was an amateur botanist and author. Engelmann's plant-hunting expeditions into the unexplored territories of the American West yielded hundreds of new discoveries.

Shaw had lofty goals in mind for his public garden: cultivating the taste of his middle-class visitors and thereby elevating society. Grove's study explains, in detail and with clarity, what this meant to someone of Shaw's day. Basing his plan on the writings of John Claudius Loudon, Shaw laid out a three-part scheme, using the gardenesque method of planting, in which ample spacing resulted in individual specimens that visitors could view from all sides.

Today, we tend to dismiss this Victorian aesthetic, but Grove believes that our prejudices have prevented a clear understanding of the influential principles that shaped landscapes such as those designed by Henry Shaw. "These early gardens and their aesthetic," she writes, "represent the culmination of a century of experimentation with new plant types and methods of planting that best displayed their unique characteristics. The profusion of color and pattern, bounded by stone walls and surrounded by countryside, juxtaposed nature and culture in a contrast as clear as that between orchids and haystacks."

Shaw's botanical garden opened to the public in June 1859, and it attracted throngs of admiring visitors. In 1867, when Shaw's attention began to turn to the creation of Tower Grove Park, he hired the English plantsman James Gurney to supervise the running of the botanical garden. Gurney's specialty was the giant *Victoria* water lily, whose gargantuan circular pads were strong enough to support a person—much to the delight of the garden's visitors. Among the many celebrities who visited over the years was Frederick Law Olmsted.

Olmsted was critical of Shaw's garden, whose style ran directly counter to his own tastes for the pastoral and the picturesque. But he was enthusiastic about the proposed adjacent park, and he wrote appreciatively of the site's "majestic simplicity of surface" and the potential for "noble breadth and delicious repose of character." For his park, however, Henry Shaw again chose to adhere to a gardenesque method, dismissing the picturesque as a style best suited to landscape painting.

In Grove's view, Shaw's choice reflected deep changes in American culture. Ideals about beauty were no longer the exclusive provenance of an elitist monopoly. The public was actively aware of the notion that aesthetics could contribute to intellectual development and moral fiber, and the refinement of taste had become a topic of widespread discussion. "The idea that the picturesque evoked nature and the gardenesque evoked art was one the viewing public could increasingly appreciate, and a distinction the park's board of commissioners clearly understood," Grove notes.

Shaw sought multiple resources in laying out his new park, visiting models throughout Europe and studying the circulation systems of Olmsted and Vaux's parks in New York City. Shaw's plan called for ten bridges, nearly seven miles of circulation routes, and a 19,500-foot hedge of American arborvitae to surround the perimeter. Twelve colorful pavilions, a sailboat pond, and mock ruins were constructed and an abundance of "the hardiest and healthiest" trees were mixed with exotic species.

Shaw's park attracted appreciative crowds, and it continues to do so today—more than a million visitors each year enjoy the "delicious repose" Olmsted predicted. Both Tower Grove Park and the neighboring Missouri Botanical Garden, which has undergone more dramatic landscape changes in the years since Shaw's death, continue to enrich lives, broaden horticultural horizons, and perhaps, even, elevate taste. The citizens of St. Louis might think fondly of Henry Shaw. It would have been a very different city without him.

The publication of *Henry Shaw's Victorian Landscapes* has been made possible by a generous gift from Jane and Joe Gleason, in loving memory of Marion and Vernon Piper. A generous grant from the Stanley Smith Horticultural Trust supported research and writing. Gifts for this project also came from the Garden Club of St. Louis and from Mr. and Mrs. Clayton Wilhite, of Ann Arbor, Michigan.

I am deeply grateful to Dr. Peter Raven, director of the Missouri Botanical Garden, for his support as we saw this book through to completion. I thank him for his thoughts on the manuscript and his foreword, which provides important context for the narrative. My thanks also go to John Karel, director of Tower Grove Park, who reviewed the manuscript and wrote an eloquent afterword to close out Shaw's story. LALH Trustee Ann D. Wilhite introduced me to these two individuals and to the wonderful institutions they oversee and acted as a guardian angel of this project from its inception.

I am pleased to have had the opportunity to work with Carol Grove, a woman of talent and intellectual conviction. Carol's fine research, sharp thinking, and strong writing skills have brought to life an important story that will contribute forcefully to a wider understanding of nineteenth-century aesthetics in America. Joel Ray, our developmental editor, was at Carol's side as she sorted her ideas. He brought support to this process and sophistication to the emerging text, which is richer for his involvement in it. Archibald Hobson also contributed to this volume's precision and readability, as did Julia Gaviria, a much valued member of the LALH editing team. This group was coordinated by Carol Betsch, whose crystalline standards for language inform every aspect of the text. I am grateful to all of them.

I thank Jonathan Lippincott for his imaginative design, his unfailing forgiveness of our many changes of mind, and his interest in and understanding of the subject of our books. It has been, and continues to be, a great pleasure to work with him. I am grateful to Jane Roy Brown, director of educational outreach for LALH, who was involved in many aspects of this book's development, and to Tanya Cushman, who provides invaluable organizational support to LALH. Douglas Holland, curator of library services and technology at the Missouri Botanical Garden, offered critical guidance and assistance. The assistance of Andrew Colligan, archivist of the Missouri Botanical Garden, was key to the illustration program of the book, to which Carol Betsch's beautiful photographs add immeasurably. The LALH publishing program continues to benefit enormously from her remarkable talent.

I am grateful to Bruce Wilcox, director of the University of Massachusetts Press, with whom we maintain a thriving partnership, and to Sally Nichols, associate production manager, and others of the Press staff, for their help at every turn. I am also grateful to the LALH advisers and the growing number of members whose gifts make our publishing program possible. My deepest thanks go to the LALH Trustees, for their unflagging commitment to our mission.

Robin Karson, Executive Director
Library of American Landscape History
Amherst, Massachusetts

Henry Shaw's Victorian Landscapes by Carol Grove is the fifth volume in the Library of American Landscape History Designers and Places Series. These richly illustrated books are published to illuminate the significance of practitioners and sites of particular importance to the field and are intended for both professional and general readers.

Library of American Landscape History, Inc., a nonprofit organization, produces books and exhibitions about North American landscape history. Its mission is to educate and thereby promote thoughtful stewardship of the land.

Foreword

When the Englishman Henry Shaw, aged eighteen years, stepped off the *Maid of Orleans* onto the levee in St. Louis in the spring of 1819, neither he nor his new associates could well have predicted what lay in store for him and for his adopted city during the next seven decades of his long and fruitful life. As we know from his own writings, he was already interested in gardening and plants; and his outstanding entrepreneurialism and business acumen enabled him to take full advantage of his new situation. Amassing a substantial fortune by the time he was forty years old, he brokered ironmongery, hardware, and other stores into a very successful business in the growing frontier town.

He was free, then, to travel in Britain and the rest of Europe. During his forties and early fifties, he took three major tours over the course of which he accumulated some of the trappings suitable for furnishing a gentleman's house. Shaw paid particular attention, as it seems, to the gardens and parks that he encountered during his travels. Once he had occupied his country house, Tower Grove, situated in the prairies about three miles beyond the edge of the city, he began to think of developing a garden or park in that vicinity and making it available for public enjoyment.

*Missouri Botanical
Garden book stamp.*

In particular, Mr. Shaw was inspired by his 1851 visit to Chatsworth, the major hereditary estate of the dukes of Devonshire. At that time, the property was being actively developed by the sixth duke and his extraordinarily talented manager, Joseph Paxton. Paxton had, that very summer, seen the Crystal Palace he had designed become the centerpiece of the expansive and memorable Great Exhibition, a sensation for all English citizens in those mid-Victorian days. What particularly seems to have affected Henry Shaw, however, were the new methods of construction that Paxton had employed not only at the Crystal Palace but in building strikingly modern glasshouses for the duke at Chatsworth—glass with few supports and an airy feeling that beautifully displayed the wonders of the botanical life that lay within. Inspired by these great works, Henry Shaw determined to have his own garden.

At first, Mr. Shaw thought of the garden essentially as a beautiful and varied display of plants. Later, under the influence of Sir William Jackson Hooker, the founding director of the Royal Botanic Gardens, Kew, as a public institution, Shaw began to think of his garden as something even greater. Advised by Dr. George Engelmann, a German obstetrician who had come to St. Louis twenty years earlier and practiced his avocation, botany, with a passion, and by Professor Asa Gray of Harvard University, the preeminent American botanist of the nineteenth century, whose counsel had been recommended by Dr. Engelmann, Mr. Shaw began to think of his creation not simply as a garden but as a *botanical* garden, where the knowledge of plants would be increased and spread throughout the world. His plantings, particularly in the systematically arranged beds to the south of the original main gate, became more synoptical and ordered, and the emphasis of the garden shifted from beauty primarily to incorporate both beauty and diversity. Mr. Shaw began to consider how his institution might conduct research, and, taking advantage of as much time as Dr. Engelmann could spare, enlisted his aid in acquiring herbarium specimens and library materials that would ultimately form the basis for that research.

A key event in the formation of the Garden's research program took place in 1880, after Henry Shaw had been directing his own garden for some twenty-one years. William Greenleaf Elliot, the chancellor of Washington University, asked that Mr. Shaw consider donating the garden and the rest of his assets to the University. Shaw decided that it should remain independent, but in 1885 he endowed a School of Botany at Washington University. The joint venture between that School and the Missouri Botanical Garden became the most active part of the emerging graduate program at Washington University, and has remained an enterprise of fundamental importance for both institutions ever since. Dr. William Trelease, a Cornell graduate who was developing a botany department at the University of Wisconsin, was recruited by Washington University in 1885, and on Mr. Shaw's death four years later, assumed the dual role of director of the Garden and professor of botany at the University. Dr. Trelease built the research program, library, and herbarium far beyond anything that could have been anticipated during Mr. Shaw's life.

Over the years, the Missouri Botanical Garden has become one of the leading botanical institutions in the world, rivaling the Royal Botanic Gardens, Kew, and The New York Botanical Garden in the breadth and strength of its worldwide reach.

In the pages of this highly informative and well-written book, Carol Grove has shed important new light on the influences that affected Henry Shaw in his planning for his botanical garden and the public park, Tower Grove Park, that he subsequently built immediately south of the Garden. Ms. Grove's scholarly research has revealed that Mr. Shaw had a very wide knowledge of the literature on landscape development and its evolution, and that he discerningly applied that knowledge in the development of both the Garden and, subsequently, the Park. In Henry Shaw's time, the botanical garden had two associated areas, a fruticetum of useful trees and shrubs immediately to the north and an arboretum forming a large adjunct to the northwest of the garden proper, which occupied just over nine acres at that time. Both the fruticetum and the arboretum were poorly maintained after Mr. Shaw's death in 1889, and more attention was focused on the garden itself. Eventually, it too was changed dramatically because of Dr. Trelease's prodding over the twenty-three years of his directorship and the eventual accession of Dr. George Moore to that office in 1912. What had begun as a very formal, traditional botanical garden then assumed the flowing lines that were prized by the end of the nineteenth century. The outlines of the modern garden, which eventually increased to comprise approximately seventy-nine acres, were laid out as the research program grew and prospered within the buildings that Mr. Shaw had constructed, and owing to the alliance with Washington University that he had forged in such a solid way. Across Magnolia Boulevard, Tower Grove Park, a lovely public park, maintained much of its original structure, but we are indebted to Carol Grove for her work, which helps us greatly to understand its gradual transition from Mr. Shaw's gardenesque style to a closer approximation of the picturesque style that it displays today.

Henry Shaw made magnificent contributions to his adopted city, and his influence continues to grow nearly 120 years after his death. Few of the great fortunes amassed in St. Louis during the nineteenth century made a lasting mark, but this enigmatic, private Yorkshireman certainly employed his to good purpose and to the benefit of a future he could only have imagined.

Professor Peter H. Raven
Director, Missouri Botanical Garden
Engelmann Professor of Botany,
Washington University in St. Louis

Acknowledgments

This book began fifteen years ago as a study of Henry Shaw's interest in British aesthetic theory. In his written plan for Tower Grove Park, Shaw had acknowledged the influence of Uvedale Price, William Gilpin, Humphry Repton, and John Claudius Loudon, and as a student new to landscape, I was intrigued why and how this transplanted Yorkshireman applied their ideas in his adopted home in the Mississippi Valley. I found that although much had been written about Shaw and his contributions to St. Louis as a benefactor and philanthropist, no one had written an in-depth assessment of his interest in landscape, the subject (I now believe) he felt most passionate about. That Shaw's original sunken parterre and herbaceous grounds had been lost to history through changes in taste only validated my interest in researching what was stored away in hundreds of linear feet of archives. Since there is no special file to refer to when documenting a landscape, I began by sorting through Shaw's papers, finding evidence woven throughout multiple leather-bound journals, in receipts from trips abroad, in his library.

Henry Shaw, advocate of landscape, took form in various ways: through sketches on the inside of a gardening encyclopedia and in his handwritten copy of Repton's epitaph recorded on the title page of the landscape gardener's collected works. His character emerged in the account book (remarkably of little interest to researchers who had come before) that recorded in meticulous detail the source, habit, and location of each plant in his botanical garden in 1859, and in his watercolor portrait (painted the same year when the garden opened) showing him standing on the grounds surrounded by conservatories and his favorite plants. By piecing together scraps of information from primary and secondary sources I began to get a sense of Henry Shaw, landscape gardener.

There are times, however, when research is trumped by serendipity, which is how I felt one dark and blustery December night as I crossed the Missouri Botanical Garden grounds. The event was a Christmas celebration at Tower Grove House, complete with a sparkling tree and carols and a visit from "Mr. Shaw" himself. Winding through the dark toward the house, I experienced what Shaw must have felt countless times when he left the city, riding out Manchester Road, down his private drive, around the grove to be welcomed at last by the lights of his country home. For one moment I saw with his eyes. Other times have not been so certain, and it is with gratitude I thank the following people, many of whom know Shaw better than I, who have helped me along the way.

First, I want to thank the many people at the Missouri Botanical Garden (past and present) who have been consistently helpful and patient, among them Brenda Sneed, Mary Stiffler, Victoria McMichael, and Martha Riley. I appreciate the botanical expertise of George Yatskievych and Norma Silber's permission to climb the tower of Tower Grove House to assess the view as Shaw did. At Tower Grove Park, I am grateful to Director John Karel for his stewardship of the park and his comments regarding the manuscript, to Sheri Pena, and to archivist Andrew Cooperman.

This project is indebted to the support and expertise of Dr. Peter H. Raven, director of the Missouri Botanical Garden, who made several rounds of helpful contributions to the manuscript. I am honored by his interest in the book. My research benefited from the ongoing support of Douglas Holland, curator of library services and technology, and Andrew Colligan, archivist, both at the Missouri Botanical Garden. They were always there to help at a moment's notice; they met deadlines with grace and are team players. I respect their knowledge of Henry Shaw, appreciate their insight and their kindness, and I owe them more than I can repay.

I appreciate the help of archivists and staff at many institutions. In England, Kate Pickard at the Royal Botanical Gardens at Kew, Pamela Taylor at Mill Hill, Ann Mitchell at Woburn, and Andrew Peppitt, the Devonshire Collection, at Chatsworth. I thank those at the Olmsted collections at the Library of Congress and at the National Park Service Frederick Law Olmsted Historic Site (Fairsted). Closer to home, I often visited Ellis Library at the University of Missouri–Columbia, the State Historical Society, and the library of the Missouri Historical Society in St. Louis.

Colleagues and students helped to shape my understanding of Shaw in the larger context of landscape history. They include members of the Alliance for Historic Landscape Preservation and those who met for conferences at the Clearing Institute, Door County, Wisconsin. In particular I thank Arnold Alanen, William Tishler, Anne Hoover, Daniel Nadenicek, Robert Harvey (who headed the 1974 Historic American Buildings Survey of Tower Grove Park) and Ian Firth. Thanks to Judith Tankard for giving me her stereo views of the garden; to colleague Terri Woods Starman, and to mentors Walter Schroeder, Susan Flader, William Biers, and Norman Land. I am particularly indebted to Patricia Crown and Osmund Overby, the professors who introduced me to landscape as a subject; I value their wisdom and friendship.

I want to acknowledge the seminal work of William Barnaby Faherty, S.J., the first historian to write at length about Henry

Shaw's life. His research and subsequent publication, *Henry Shaw: His Life and Legends,* is the standard text on the subject, and provided a foundation to work from. My copy is worn and filled with notes. When I purchased it directly from the University of Missouri Press (their last copy), I found it inscribed with his signature and "good wishes from the author"; I have always considered that a sign of encouragement.

I am most grateful to Robin Karson, executive director of the Library of American Landscape History, who responded to my letter insisting that Shaw's legacy was worthy of publication. She has been diplomatic, patient, and encouraging throughout this long process. I appreciate very much the help of other people associated with this project: Ann Wilhite, her early and ongoing enthusiasm and support, Joel Ray, his vital role in shaping the manuscript, Jonathan Lippincott, Archibald Hobson, Jane Roy Brown, Jane Henderson, and especially Carol Betsch, her photographs of garden and park and her help weaving together the verbal and the visual.

I humbly thank my family for their support—my husband, Bob, our remarkable children, Tony and Lilli, Dora, and my mother, Jean. Lastly, I want to thank my father, Allen Jack Edwards, scholar and mentor, who has looked over my shoulder throughout. This work is dedicated to his memory.

Henry Shaw's Victorian Landscapes

Introduction

Henry Shaw's friend and botanical adviser George Engelmann once excitedly called St. Louis the "center of North America, if not the world and civilization." Shaw shared his enthusiasm; practically from his arrival in the spring of 1819, he envisioned the city's potential, and he would contribute to its progress—in education, science, politics, social service, and aesthetics—until his death in 1889. During his lifetime he gave to St. Luke's Hospital, Christ Church Cathedral, and the Missouri School for the Blind; in his will he named as beneficiaries institutions including the Home of the Friendless and the Little Sisters of the Poor. He helped to found the Missouri Historical Society and the Mercantile Library, was founder of the School of Botany at Washington University, and endowed scholarships for practical gardeners. His contributions to the city were more than monetary: he adorned the walls of a local hospital with artwork purchased abroad; he donated land for an orphanage but also made Christmas visits to the children there. Shaw believed in education and opportunity, better services for the disadvantaged, and the importance of cultural institutions as a means of improving the city.

Henry Shaw,
1800–1889.

This concern for civic improvement is evident in Shaw's most important personal projects, the Missouri Botanical Garden and Tower Grove Park. His decision to create a public garden and park went far beyond an interest in providing St. Louis with pleasant surroundings. More important, both institutions were vehicles for elevating its citizens. Foremost in his mind was the belief that the cultivation of taste—the appreciation of nature, art, and beauty—could act as a powerful instrument of reform.[1] Not only could it educate and refine, it could shape a person's judgment, and the development of critical perception could ultimately raise the level of society as a whole. Shaw understood that addressing taste was as important as considering economics, practicality, and the needs of the city's future in a given project. He viewed the botanical garden and "park keeping" as key instruments in making the citizens of St. Louis more discriminating and civilized, and the city a better place in which to live.

Shaw's interest in this particular kind of improvement may date to his earliest days in St. Louis, when the city was an outpost and busy shipping port and there was a clear divide between the rough and the refined. It may also date to his childhood and adolescence in Sheffield, England, where he saw a similar contrast between factory workers and the landed gentry and aristocracy who lived in the countryside. Certainly his interest manifested the collective concern with social and intellectual improvement that shaped the middle classes of both his country of birth and his country of choice. And it was no doubt the natural outgrowth of his own education in taste, by way of extensive European travel and reading, which came after several decades of concentrating—to the exclusion of virtually everything else—on business.

Shaw's belief that the discernment acquired through an appreciation for aesthetics could teach and shape individuals coalesced most powerfully in his interest in "garden botany"—the science of plants—and the art of design. He enjoyed personally arranging gardens and grounds, collecting exotic plants, and drawing plans. With age and insight he understood that he could make a unique and vital contribution to society by labeling trees and shrubs and promoting an interest in flowers and vines organized in botanical sequence. This combination of art and science at the garden was intended to aid in the development of "higher tastes and manners," and to benefit "all classes of society."[2] Likewise, Tower Grove Park would not only ornament the city, it would be conducive to health and happiness, and promote "the advancement of refinement and culture."[3]

Henry Shaw's life spanned the nineteenth century, from 1800 to 1889, yet figuratively he stood with one foot planted in the eigh-

teenth century, the other firmly in the nineteenth. He was representative of two periods of history both in his personal interests
and in relation to the characteristics that define each age. Shaw
inherited many of the sensibilities and traditions prevalent in the
eighteenth century: he was a gentleman in demeanor and way of
life, educated and well read, and as he traveled he acquired art,
furnishings, clothing, and wine, developed an interest in architecture, and became a deeply engaged advocate of landscape. When
having his likeness painted, he chose the tradition of eighteenth-
century portraiture—incorporating objects that reveal the sitter's
interests within the composition—to express himself. In the management of his estate he adopted an aristocratic sense of duty and
a commitment to accountability and productivity.

Shaw was well suited to the image of the gentleman gardener,
a station associated with an earlier age that combined privilege
with specialized knowledge. In the nineteenth century, however,
the role of the gentleman gardener diminished, and responsibility
was increasingly transferred to hands-on gardeners trained in
what was becoming an increasingly popular profession. A gentleman gardener who involved himself in every aspect of planting,
nurturing, and design, Shaw gracefully represents the moment in
history when privilege made way for middle-class interests, and in
this way he personifies the Victorian age. An interest in innovation, education, and improvement of the landscape and society as
a whole mark him as representative of the nineteenth century. At-
tuned to the concerns of the working middle class, and to democratic aspiration, he believed the enjoyment of nature to be a path
to societal reform. He embraced technological progress and improved methods in gardening, choosing to be guided by contemporary models and writings rather than historical ones.

Shaw returned to England both before and after he became a
naturalized U.S. citizen on July 3, 1843, and he retained an affinity for his native country. Throughout his life, his preference for
English objects, conventions, and ideas persisted. When choosing
garden seats and urns, for example, he ordered from the foundry

at Coalbrookdale, considered the birthplace of the Industrial Revolution. The tiles he chose to ornament the front hall of his town house were from Stoke-on-Trent. At midcentury he still signed his name with the title of "Esquire," evoking the English landed gentry. His friend Thomas Dimmock's biographical sketch emphasized Shaw's ideological relationship to England, evident in his interest in retaining the English "hereditary traits" and the habits he was born with.[4] He preferred to be surrounded by the things that reminded him of England: his town house and country villa at Tower Grove were filled with older English furniture, the pictures and prints on the walls were of English subjects, and he "preferred to read his favorite authors in the English editions, through which he first knew them." Although Shaw chose to live in America, and absorbed an American point of view that balanced his Englishness, his attachment for the land of his birth remained deep and ardent.

Shaw's memory of and respect for England also shaped his work at his garden and park. Visually and ideologically English references abound: his early plant houses resemble those at the Sheffield Botanic Garden, and his park maze was modeled on that at Hampton Court. He used English practitioners and authors as the basis for his work, in particular Joseph Paxton and John Claudius Loudon,[5] whom Shaw placed on a par with the eighteenth-century botanist Linnaeus and naturalist Alexander von Humboldt. To Shaw, who could read French and Italian, choosing English references was a deliberate act rather than done for ease and convenience. Shaw's ultimate inspiration was Chatsworth, in Derbyshire, which had long been recognized as one of the most distinguished estates in England. Maintaining an efficient and profitable estate was considered the moral responsibility of the English landed gentry, and Shaw's decision to shape his own property was a reference to this tradition. Yet when he visited Chatsworth in 1851, the estate was becoming known for more contemporary projects—an arboretum and a world-class collection of orchids and water lilies—joint efforts of Paxton and the duke of Devonshire. These were the projects that galvanized him.

Never marrying and without children, Shaw viewed his villa, and ultimately his park and garden, as a legacy in lieu of the family he did not have and as the hallmark of dignity in place of the ancestry he lacked. Shaw's choice of Chatsworth as a model for his own "ancestral" home and grounds may reflect an affinity he perceived between himself and the sixth duke of Devonshire (1790–1858). Growing up not far from Chatsworth, Shaw knew of William Spencer Cavendish and likely viewed him, and his circumstances, with admiration. Of the same generation (Cavendish was ten years older than Shaw), both had reserved personalities yet were eager to share their ideas and enthusiasm with people of all positions and rank. Cavendish would inherit both title and property at the age of twenty-one on the death of his father; Henry Shaw, "Esquire," would work to acquire the American equivalent. Both men were "bit by gardening" and aware of its contribution to society, and that neither married allowed each to devote his time to projects too demanding for one with family responsibilities. The home and landscape of the "Bachelor Duke" were the abiding loves of Cavendish's life,[6] and the same can be said of Shaw, who in old age would refer to his plants as his family, in need of nurturing.

Henry Shaw's garden and park were a manifestation of a growing public interest in botany, which had begun in the eighteenth century. Discoveries that resulted from voyages of exploration prompted curiosity about plants and encouraged the collection of exotic specimens from the far corners of the world. Gentlemen connoisseurs and amateur scientists were the first to be drawn to this field of inquiry, but as the eighteenth century progressed the subject was no longer reserved for specialists, becoming more accessible, in part, because of the system of plant classification devised by Linnaeus. The well-read and well-to-do indulged their new interest in plants by reading descriptive books on the subject; it became a major topic of conversation in cultivated drawing rooms. Poetry such as Erasmus Darwin's 1789 *Loves of the Plants* (which Henry Shaw owned), which combined the scientific language of botany with references to human sexuality, made for popular, and controversial, reading. Botany also became fashionable in the decorative arts: prints and paintings of exotic specimens, similar to those in Robert Thornton's *Temple of Flora* (1799), hung on walls papered with botanical motifs. Gardens and conservatories included a steadily widening range of plants, their hot colors and unusual shapes contrasting with plants native to the site. Entire collections of a given type were prized; for ex-

Title page and frontispiece from Henry Shaw's copy of Erasmus Darwin's Loves of the Plants *(1789).*

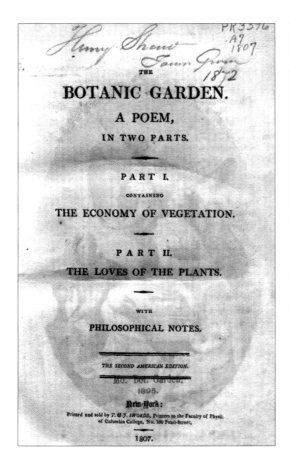

"Botanizing" at the Missouri Botanical Garden, 1890.

ample, collections of ericaceous plants called "American gardens" could be found across England.

In the nineteenth century the capacity of botany to teach and reform made it a proper hobby for an increasingly broad audience including women and young children. What had been a scholarly, then a genteel, interest became a widespread phenomenon among the working class. The study of plants and their collection, called "botanizing," prompted the formation of botanical clubs that organized excursions and fieldwork. Interest was no longer limited to exotic specimens brought from afar; amateur collectors were drawn to the native plants that could be gathered nearby. Scrutinizing mosses, dissecting flowers, and organizing flowering plants by petal color became popular activities (Shaw himself made scrapbooks of pressed flowers for two young ladies who lived near him in the city). Magazines such as *Godey's Lady's Book* published articles entitled "Botany as a Study for Young Ladies" and "The Collection and Preservation of Plants," and children learned the subject in textbooks such as Asa Gray's *Botany for Young People and Common Schools* (1858). Soon amateur botany would evolve into a broader field of interest, referred to as "Nature-Study" by the horticulturalist Liberty Hyde Bailey and his contemporaries, which taught youngsters to appreciate the whole of the environment.

The popularity of botany was fueled in part by the nineteenth-century spirit of reform. Botanizing combined physical exercise with the gathering of practical knowledge, promoted intellectual development by improving one's ability to observe and classify information, and enhanced mental discipline by improving memory and reasoning.[7] It added not only to personal knowledge but to the country's knowledge of its own natural history. Contemporary sources praised the characteristic that Henry Shaw appreciated most: botany's ability to promote gentility—refinement, respectability, and politeness—characteristics necessary for a cultivated life. The study of botany was seen as a means of improving the young and the poor, of making wiser people and better citizens, of elevating society. It was in this nineteenth-century context of reform and education that botany, the science that combined "pleasure with improvement,"[8] had its greatest impact.

Henry Shaw remained intimately engaged at his garden and park until his death at eighty-nine years of age, even handling the payroll personally until one month before he died. Seeing the public enjoy and learn at the garden and park was his "bright and unfailing pleasure."[9] For forty years, he could, from the tower of his villa, take in the garden's parterres and observation tower to the north or work being done in the kitchen gardens to the south; in the distance he could distinguish the trees and drives of Tower Grove Park. His appreciation for parks as vehi-

View north from Tower Grove House through the grove toward the conservatory, 1900.

cles of social reform, his understanding of the needs and workings of St. Louis, his concern for "economy," and his deep interest in botany, aesthetics, and the gardenesque method shaped the sweep of prairie he had purchased nearly fifty years earlier. After he was gone many would remember the enthusiasm and style with which Henry Shaw had lived, including the celebration on his eighty-first birthday, when he illuminated the garden with Japanese hanging lanterns and ornamented Tower Grove House by spelling out in vivid red flowers the word *Salve*—Latin for "welcome."

1

"An Open and Undulating Half Prairie, Half Shrubbery"

FROM SHEFFIELD TO TOWER GROVE

Trade, all travel to the far West, whether for pleasure or for scientific research, . . . made St. Louis the starting point and base of operations.

—HIRAM M. CHITTENDEN, Captain, Corps of Engineers, in *The American Fur Trade of the Far West* (1902)

At the turn of the nineteenth century, Henry Shaw's birthplace, Sheffield, England, was responding to change brought about by the Industrial Revolution. The coalfields of South Yorkshire had been mined for centuries, and Sheffield now profited from the increased production of fine cutlery and tools such as knives, shovels, axes, and saws which earned it a worldwide reputation. The year Shaw was born (1800) Sheffield had 31,000 inhabitants, and it would grow by 40 percent between 1820 and 1830. The "advancing tide of brick and mortar"[1] was also apparent at such nearby industrial cities as Leeds, Manchester, and Liverpool. But Sheffield, referred to as "a dark picture in a golden frame," exemplified the increasing contrast of nature and industry. Surrounding the smoke of the city were suburban garden plots tended for pleasure rather than profit and an unspoiled landscape that contrasted dramatically with the world of manufacturing and production. To the west were the crags and hills of the Peak District; to the south, the river Derwent spilled over the picturesque cliffs of Matlock Bath; and in neighboring Derbyshire there was the great park of the Chatsworth estate.

At Chatsworth, the ancestral home of the Cavendish family and the dukes of Devonshire, 1,000 acres of parkland and 105 acres of gardens surrounded the house. A monument to classicism, it had been altered and enlarged over centuries, and its vast grounds incorporated every phase of garden style, from the formal parterres of the seventeenth-century horticulturalist George London to Lancelot "Capability" Brown's deer parks to Joseph Paxton's botanical innovations begun in the 1830s. Industrial Sheffield and the broad sweep of the grounds at Chatsworth were the highly contrasting landscapes Henry Shaw knew as a growing boy. These environs, along with the grounds of Mill Hill, the secondary school he attended outside London, framed his vision and perception. They served as clear contrasts to the landscape of the American prairie he would settle in as a young man. Later in life, when Shaw began to formulate his own ideas for garden and park, he would refer to these landscapes again, by comparison and for inspiration.

Henry was born to Joseph Shaw and Sarah Hoole Shaw on July 24, 1800. He, his parents, and two younger sisters, Sarah and Caroline, lived in the hilly northwestern district of Sheffield referred to as Netherthorpe; nearby, the river Don on the north connected with the town's namesake, the river Sheaf, from the south. To the east was Green Lane, adjacent a stream lined with cottage gardens, and Henry's father's place of employment. Joseph Shaw, a native of the town of Leicester almost seventy miles to the south, had come to Sheffield sometime before 1800 and, with a partner, Robert Jobson, ran the Green Lane Works, a manufacturer of stoves, grates, and fireplace equipment.

The potential for the elder Shaw to become a merchant-capitalist by marketing the goods he produced was great. So, too, was the pressure to become a success like the members of his wife's family who had proved themselves in manufacturing, merchandising, and local politics. Indeed, the middle-class circumstances Sarah was comfortable with may have tested Joseph Shaw. She had come from a prominent local family, and one senses that Joseph had married "up" to a position he was ultimately unable to maintain. Little is known of Joseph's background and he appears to have been little more than a figurehead in his family. Henry doubted that his father would ever accomplish anything positive in his life and one suspects that he took after his mother in matters of taste and ambition. His parents' relationship, which was undermined by Joseph's lack of business acumen and flight from responsibility when he left England for America in 1818, may have influenced Henry's decision to remain single for life.

As a young boy, Shaw attended school in the nearby village of Thorn, just north of Sheffield. When time came for his secondary education to begin at age eleven, Shaw was sent to Mill Hill, an all-male private school north of London. Opened in 1807, less than five years before Shaw's arrival, the school was established by Nonconformist ("dissenting") merchants and ministers for the sons of Presbyterians, Congregationalists, and Baptists (such as Henry's father)—those who practiced a faith outside the Church of England. Its rural location was chosen as protection against the physical and moral dangers of city life found in London and, increasingly, in industrial towns such as Sheffield. Although the institution was new, its site was one of historical importance, on a transportation route used by Romans, Saxons, and Normans. Its ridge-top location provided panoramas of Epping Forest, the North Downs, and the town of Harrow.

Some graduates of the school went on to careers in law, education, and the church. Other students would pattern themselves after the school's merchant founders and enter into the newer (and somewhat less respectable) realm of commerce, trading in the manufactured goods born of the Industrial Revolution; education in a private institution such as Mill Hill could provide the polish and enlightenment necessary to distinguish a would-be merchant from his competition. As a Millhillian, Shaw took courses in the classics, composition, and French, and accounts suggest that he was an unremarkable (though well-mannered) student. Of the standard subjects, fluency in the French language and math would turn out to be the most applicable later in life; but it appears that from early on Shaw preferred growing pinks and geraniums to learning Euclidean geometry and Greek, and that he sought out quiet corners half-hidden by vines and flowers as places for study. For a student drawn more to flora than philosophy, the physical environment of the Mill Hill grounds proved to be an ideal place to nurture an interest in the science of nature.

Mill Hill and Botanical Exchange

Mill Hill was located on the site of Ridgeway House, previously the home of the eighteenth-century Quaker Peter Collinson (1694–1768), who had ornamented the place with a collection of stately trees and a garden that reflected his interest in botany.[2] Collinson's garden of American plants was famous throughout England, as was his collection of cedar, cypress, and sycamore trees, many given as mementos by friends. He corresponded with Linnaeus on botanical matters and was a principal figure in the establishment of plant trade between England and America, pioneering in the exchange of exotics. He was responsible for introducing more than two hundred species of plants to England, and his collected seeds were traded and dispersed throughout the country. On his property Collinson experimented with the propagation of plants, testing their ability to thrive outside their native habitat, and created a noteworthy collection of botanical specimens. In 1835, sixty-seven years after Collinson's death, the horticultural expert John Claudius Loudon, who would be an important influence on Shaw, visited Mill Hill. Loudon's account of the gardens there, published in his *Arboretum et Fruticetum Britanicum* three years later, documented the collection of foreign and native trees on the site, several of which still ornament the school grounds today.[3] This most formative period of Shaw's education was spent at a place rich in associations with botany, and the image of an impressionable Henry taking lessons in the very quarters inhabited years before by a pioneer in the field of botanical discovery anticipates his later work.[4]

The botanical reciprocity Collinson helped establish was a product of voyages of discovery that began encircling the globe in the second half of the eighteenth century. Unknown corners of the world were investigated by global pioneers such as James Cook, who sailed to the South Seas in 1768, and others who helped map territory and assess an array of data and material culture from around the world. Such vigorous and focused adventure provided so much new material that it was necessary to produce encyclopedic treatments of all that had become available.[5] Joseph Banks, the English naturalist who became unofficial director of the royal gardens at Kew after his return from voyages abroad with Cook in 1771, introduced plants from Australia and China. Linnaeus, who created the binomial system of nomenclature (designating plants and animals with a two-part name, the first word of which is the genus, and the second, together with the name of the genus, designating a particular species), helped fix and order botanical knowledge. Alexander von Humboldt, who studied the earth and its properties, such as atmosphere, magnetic fields, and barometric pressure, explored widely and made people acquainted with the incredible richness of tropical life. This immense growth of knowledge continued to influence and shape life in the nineteenth century through a second generation of radical thinkers and explorers who carried on the process: Charles Darwin, Joseph Dalton Hooker, and the explorer Alfred Russel Wallace, to name only a few.

Of the resources that were identified and claimed during exploration, plants were an important component, and botany as a science would benefit greatly. The 1799–1804 South American expedition of Humboldt and Aimé Bonpland, for example, had doubled the number of plants known to the western world. The

French botanist André Michaux (1746–1802) had collected timber and medicinal plants in eastern North America, sending them to the official French institution, the Jardin des Plantes, in Paris.[6] Specimens were obtained from all corners of the world, and their cultivation drastically increased the number of plants known and made available. The palette of colors expanded to include hot oranges, reds, and fuchsia, which contrasted strongly with the softer hues of native plants. In England, aristocratic collectors financed trips for the sake of obtaining seeds, cones, and root systems to complement their private collections. The interest in plant collecting was facilitated by the Wardian case, invented in 1829 by Nathaniel Bagshaw Ward as a means of transporting plants long distances; large, enclosed cases created self-sustaining microenvironments, enabling plants to withstand extended periods without cultivation. More refined versions, later referred to as terrariums,

Examples of Wardian cases used to ship plants from Australia to St. Louis.

decorated parlors into the twentieth century. The nineteenth-century middle-class interest in horticulture grew in part from this ability to make exotic specimens available. Facilitated also by the new genre of horticultural journalism, the popularity of gardening as a pastime spread quickly to America. Botanists and plant traders expanded the sphere of communication, and the seeds and plants themselves, to the western hemisphere.

A key part of the network that brought popular botany to America was Peter Collinson's collaboration with the pioneer botanist and explorer John Bartram (1699–1777) of Philadelphia. The two exchanged seeds—Collinson brokered them for Bartram in London—increasing the diversity not only of their own gardens but of collections on both sides of the Atlantic. Bartram's garden, dating to 1728, included both ornamental and economic plants (those of practical usefulness), and was considered the "Botanic Garden of America" in the colonial period. His success as an exporter can be attributed to a simple practice: by first cultivating plants, he gave them a head start prior to shipment, thus avoiding the losses normally experienced in transport. Bartram's exchanges introduced a large number of new species into cultivation, some planted at Peter Collinson's garden at Ridgeway House. Shaw's schooling at Mill Hill, on the site of these plantings, enabled him to observe the rewards of the pioneering Collinson-Bartram partnership and experience the product of botanical exchange firsthand, at an early age. He would continue this tradition years later, sending a western pinyon pine, *Pinus edulis*, which bears edible seeds within its cones, to director William Jackson Hooker for the arboretum at Kew.

Shaw's Fortunes in North America

Henry Shaw and his father left England for North America in June 1818, crossing the Atlantic and landing in Quebec. Joseph

Shaw hoped to escape his debts in England and find new opportunities abroad; Henry sensed adventure, and the opportunity to make his own fortune. When they arrived the two went separate ways. Henry headed south through the Hudson River valley to Manhattan, then continued by boat to the port of New Orleans. There he would learn the cotton trade, and he planned to save his father's abortive attempt at importing: Joseph and an acquaintance from Tennessee had shipped goods from England, but their products sat in the port, without a buyer, until Henry intervened. Whether from poor judgment, bad business sense, or lack of follow-through, Joseph failed not only at this venture but repeatedly in others (although he was successful in fleeing from creditors in England and from the brother-in-law who served as guarantor for borrowed funds). From their arrival in North America, Henry proved himself the antithesis of his father in business dealings; for each of Joseph Shaw's miscalculations, Henry had multiple successes.

While his father stayed in Canada, Henry decided to head up the Mississippi River. Just two years before, the *Zebulon Pike* had successfully navigated all the way to St. Louis, farther upriver than any steamboat before. The advent of steam power enabled goods to be shipped efficiently both north and west via the confluence of the Mississippi and Missouri Rivers, just above the city. Hoping to capitalize on the business opportunities made possible by this new route and method of transportation, and suspecting his fluency in French would be an asset as it had been in Louisiana, Shaw left on the *Maid of New Orleans* in the spring of 1819. Along the route, the adventurous eighteen-year-old mentally recorded the experience: the bluffs at Vicksburg, a Cherokee who swam past the lumbering steamboat, and his fellow travelers.[7] Nearing the port he noted scenes of domesticity such as fruit trees in bloom and pleasant houses, a contrast to the old oaks and landscape of Louisiana.

On May 3 Shaw arrived in St. Louis, joining nearly four thousand Indian traders, settlers from Kentucky, Virginia, and other parts of the South, and the French citizens whose families had established the village a generation before. To a young man who had left a cultivated life an ocean away, St. Louis must have appeared promising yet forbidding: it was at once a "scene of bright prospect" and the rough western frontier of the nation.[8] The town that had been founded by Pierre Laclede and Auguste Chouteau as a wilderness outpost and center of fur trade for the Mississippi Valley in 1764 was growing at a fast pace.[9] Communal farm fields were being platted and few traces of the French colonial town, picturesque but disorderly by some observations, remained. The early town had been replaced by a grid of streets, increasingly known by their English equivalents rather than their original French names, which ran inland from the waterfront, and by an expanding network of neighborhoods, mercantile blocks, and churches (including a cathedral).[10]

This physical transformation met the growing needs of a population of newcomers seeking the same kind of opportunities Shaw sought. The Mississippi River was no longer perceived as a boundary but rather as the point of departure for western expansion. Americans, French, and increasing numbers of Germans and Irish formed the expanding economic base of the city. River

"Our City," *an aerial view of the St. Louis levee and the Mississippi River.* Lithograph by A. Janicke & Co., St. Louis; published by Hagen & Pfau, 1859.

trade and steamboat traffic were rapidly expanding; assemblages
of keelboats and fleets of steam ferries lined the landing for a
mile. Contemporaries who described the dust and bustle of commerce remarked on the piles of produce, the many wholesale gro-
cery stores, and the walls of warehouses on the dirt or mud banks
of the wharf, all jostling for space. The city radiated outward
from the river, beyond the western fringe, into the wider setting,
and observers were struck by the "scramble for the almost limit-
less West . . . spread out before one's vision."[11]

Shaw spent the next five years in business travel north and
south, from Montreal to New Orleans, much of it by means of the
river. This proved a wise and profitable business move. His markets were geographically and economically diverse: he provided
precision implements to the Western territory, to military posts in
Wisconsin, Michigan, and Iowa, and to markets to the south in
the Ozarks. His customer base was a disparate combination of
pioneer farmers, fur traders, military outfits, and more genteel
types. Shaw dabbled in the trade of goods grown or obtained lo-
cally, such as cotton, flour, and furs, but the quality goods he imported from England provided his initial financial success. He
quickly established himself as the premier hardware importer of

*St. Louis from the
Mississippi River.*
From Harper's Weekly
Supplement, *New York.*

the region, and his advertisements indicate a varied stock of other English goods—not only tools but flannel, bleach, dry goods, and transferware dishes, the best "queensware" he could obtain from Liverpool.

By late 1824, St. Louis had become Shaw's hub and home, not so much by conscious decision as by resignation. The city's geographical situation, which ensured it a role as an ideal and profitable distribution center, contributed greatly to his success. He thought of, and wrote about, going to other places and climates—Nashville, Louisville, and locations farther away such as Canada, Germany—and even of return to England in the future. He lamented that New Orleans weather was better for his health than the cold farther north, although the yellow fever epidemic in the South tempered his sentiments. Ultimately, Shaw chose the river town of St. Louis over the bayous of Louisiana for his home. As an astute businessman, he could not pass up the opportunity there, even though conditions were different the year he arrived. A financial depression hit. Money was tight, and city lots and thousands of acres of land were being foreclosed on. Shaw, however, astutely saw the potential of buying city and country land that was lost to debt or nonpayment of taxes, and began to keep an eye out for such property.

Weekly rides—ostensibly to survey land for purchase but also because he loved being on horseback and experiencing a countryside so different from that of England—took Shaw to the vast acreage beyond the outskirts of the city. On one such occasion he visited a particular sweep of prairie to the southwest, about three miles from the city center, which bounded the French colonial common fields. La Prairie de la Barrière à Denoyer, so named perhaps in reference to a local gatekeeper, Louis Denoyer, was a two-mile stretch of fertile land, devoid of trees except for a handful of cottonwoods and clumps of hazel bushes. A shallow watercourse, dotted with native water lilies, crossed the gentle rise of ground grown over with tall bluestem prairie grass and adorned with occasional patches of wild strawberry.[12] Only a narrow road passed through the property; there were no houses in sight. Twenty years later this land would become Shaw's estate, and eventually, the Missouri Botanical Garden and Tower Grove Park.

At twenty-five years of age, Shaw was absorbed in business. By his own admission, he paid little attention to politics and showed no interest in having a social life. (According to later contemporaries, he was quite reserved, and historians have referred to him as elusive and enigmatic.) Initially, in his first rudimentary warehouse space, owned by the merchants Edward Tracy and Charles Wahrendorff at 4 North Main Street, he lived, cooked, and sold in a single room. He kept copious notes on modes of transportation and on his percentage of profits, recording his stock in triplicate. He expanded his business to include the export of lead (and later cotton and beeswax) in exchange for the goods he imported for sale, bypassing the need for cash transactions. He continued to give attention and financial help to his mother and sisters, who left their home in Sheffield and relocated in Pittsford, New York, near Rochester, and he repaid his father's debts to family members back in England. In Canada and the northern territory, his father continued to look for opportunity, moving from one unsuccessful scheme to another, until finally joining the family in New York. As long as three years would pass between letters to his son (in one case, he said, studying the Bible kept him too busy to write); when he did communicate, he tried to pressure Henry into more of what the younger Shaw called "mismanaged speculations."

Henry kept to his own expanding business. He moved from the warehouse and opened his own store up the street at 58 North Main, near the homes of important citizens and future business associates William Clark and Pierre and Auguste Chouteau, whose family had helped found the city. As profits grew, so did Shaw's needs and plans for the future. He purchased his first slave and expanded the number and type of goods he handled, entering the fur trade. His sister Caroline had begun to think all three of the siblings might remain unmarried, and questioned the

Henry Shaw at thirty-five years of age.

reason for Henry's reticence, wondering, "Is it true, that 'business gentlemen' mingle very little with society until they have accumulated a fortune?"[13] But about this time Shaw wrote to his sister Sarah that he was looking for a wife—countless good qualities and a handsome dowry were among the requirements.

Not only was he thinking about a wife, he was beginning to consider a different life altogether—one not driven by the sale of anvils, bits, and chisels. The business he was so adept at was a means of supporting himself and his family, a way to prove he wasn't plagued by his father's weaknesses, and perhaps most importantly the means to engage in the life he really wanted. Shaw spent the next several years considering his options. One idea he entertained early on, suggested in a letter he sent Sarah in 1832, was to sell his import business. He was beginning to buy property—city lots in St. Louis and a few in Rochester as well. Importing seemed less profitable than property, which could generate income and grow in value. In May, two years later, Shaw once again wrote about selling the business and this time mentioned plans to travel to Europe. In the fall of 1835, his family moved into a comfortable brick house in Rochester that he had built for them.

By January 1839, Shaw was getting closer to acting on his new plans. He inventoried his assets, which included exactly $47,678.39 in merchandise, $15,766.08 in gold and silver, $92,575.68 in bonds and mortgages for money lent, and $33,923.11 in property—a total of $189,943.26. He had prospered from the import-export business, and he had used his income to purchase real estate and to lend money, often with mortgages as collateral. He was now receiving rents from commercial and residential properties he owned. The roster of those he had lent money included anonymous persons and prominent citizens. He lent Meriwether Lewis Clark $8,500; Scruggs-Vandervoort-Barney, the mercantile establishment that would become a St. Louis institution, borrowed funds. The largest individual debt, of $18,543.55, was owed by Thomas Jefferson Payne, and it was secured by his Prairie des Noyers land (as it came to be known) southwest of the city. Shaw could sense social and economic changes that would affect business as he had known it. Importation from England had slowed, and the railroad (first chartered in Missouri in 1837) would soon replace transportation by river. Moreover, the city was increasingly split by the clash of feelings that would lead to the Civil War (the war itself would cut it off and starve its economy). Even the local labor force would change. Slaves, including the eleven Shaw then owned, were being replaced by immigrants, many of them German, who were arriving in great numbers.[14]

Shaw the Gentleman

The $22,876.34 Shaw cleared in 1839 alone was, in his opinion, more than any man in his circumstances ought to make in a single year.[15] With such profits, and with the income his property ensured, he was confident enough to make the change he had thought about for a decade. He turned over his accounts and assets, including bonds, notes, and cash, to a local businessman and friend, Peter Lindell, and the law firm of Spaulding and Tiffany, who acted as his agents. This major transition left Shaw free of the day-to-day handling of business matters. With the ability to keep in touch through his agents, his uncle in London, and his family, he could implement his plan of traveling to Europe. In July 1840, his affairs in order, he left St. Louis, heading first to Rochester to visit with his family. Then he and Caroline, who accompanied him on the first leg of the trip, sailed toward England.

Guided by his middle-aged interests and those of a new man of leisure, Shaw began a decade of intermittent travel. In the eighteenth-century tradition of the Grand Tour, his extended travels to England, the Continent, and Asia Minor allowed him the opportunity to experience as a gentleman the arts, culture, and social and intellectual stimulation. These tours provided him the occasion to collect objects he loved—art, furniture, clothing—and to educate his taste. He collected ideas as well, by means of firsthand experience, by communicating with people from other cultures, and by the acquisition of books for his personal library. Trading the life of a businessman for that of a gentleman also allowed him the time to discern new interests. It was during this ten-year period of travel that Shaw exchanged his enthusiasm for adding figures and calculating profits for an enthusiasm for gardening. A passion for plants would grab hold of him, and, with time, consume him.

The first extended tour, in 1840–42, was grand in every respect. Shaw visited Sheffield, Oxford, and London, spent Christmas in Florence and New Year's Eve in Paris, and continued eastward through Geneva, Venice, and the Ionian Islands to Smyrna in Asia Minor (now İzmir, Turkey), stopping in Constantinople (modern Istanbul), and then returned through Milan and Vienna to England. His sister Caroline went with him as far as Ireland and England, and he also traveled with friends such as the young Charles Chouteau, of St. Louis, with whom he toured France and Italy, or with guides, such as the Greek traveling companion Demosthenes Simos, who helped negotiate local customs and unfamiliar landscapes. Shaw's practice of keeping meticulous records has left a trail of receipts and communications that reveal his accommodations, where he dined, what he drank, and the modes of transportation he used. His activities were those of a gentleman and a tourist: he stared into the crater at Vesuvius, arranged for apartments in St. Petersburg, took Italian language lessons in the Campagna, and signed an agreement for a barge trip on the Nile. To Shaw, the Schönbrunn Palace in Vienna was as beautiful as the Sistine Chapel, Ireland as memorable as the Ionian Islands, the waterfalls of Wales's Mt. Snowdon on horseback as enticing as an evening at the Paris Opéra in evening dress.

Purchases Shaw made while traveling reveal his level of sophistication and taste. He bought mosaics from S. Barberi in Rome and a pastel drawing by Fantin-Latour from the art dealer Durand-Ruel in Paris, had garments tailored in Trieste and jewelry made in Vienna. Like Humphry Repton, the landscape gardener whose work he read, he had a penchant for crimson Moroccan leather, which he used to embellish mahogany chairs. A variety of art decorated his surroundings: an Italian landscape by Rosa de Tivoli and a valuable oil painting of "Susanna and the Elders" hung in his office. He reportedly bought a Madonna by Annibale Carracci for his sister. He tasted, and purchased, spirits for drink and dining: his wine cellar stored thousands of bottles of both European and American varieties. He was egalitarian in his choices; he enjoyed Jamaican rum, French champagne, St. Louis beer, and Spanish sherry (for which the large amounts purchased suggest a preference). As he traveled he bought books for his collection, written in English, French, Italian, Latin, and German on a variety of subjects—history, business, and the arts—which he would organize in his library by language.

When Shaw returned to St. Louis in the fall of 1842, he scrambled to take care of personal and business matters so he could leave again by the following summer. During the few months he was in the city, he turned control of some of his business interests over to Caroline, who had just moved to St. Louis from Rochester, and to whom he assigned power of attorney. In her brother's absence she collected rents (and reportedly was a sensitive landlord), managing hundreds of lots and acres on his behalf, and kept an eye out for property to purchase.

The personal business Shaw attended to during these months reveals his frame of mind and his fully conscious decision to make St. Louis his permanent home. In particular, he oversaw the purchase of hundreds of arpents of land southwest of the city, the Prairie des Noyers, which he had admired on horseback twenty years before and which would become his estate, Tower Grove;[16] he purchased fruit trees to be planted there, an act of faith and commitment to the future for all gardeners, especially new ones; and he became a U.S. citizen. In April 1843 he received a book from an important British author, John Claudius Loudon, that would prove to be a valuable reference in shaping the vast acreage outside the city.[17] The work addressed planting arboretum-like settings and dealt with the preservation of large areas of ground near cities which could be used for various purposes, including parks. Its acquisition marks the beginning of Shaw's active interest in planting and planning landscapes, which would give focus to his upcoming trip.

Shaw left in July 1843 on his second Grand Tour, beginning in England and Scotland. These return visits, to landscapes he was familiar with, helped cultivate his appreciation for the varied sensations they could provide. Guided by his copy of William Gilpin's tour books, which educate the reader on the subject of beauty in nature, Shaw saw how different feelings are evoked by the sublime, the beautiful, and the picturesque in natural and cultivated settings.[18] On the other hand, assorted institutions along the route—the Royal Botanic Garden at Kew, near London, the botanical garden at Glasgow, and the Sheffield Botanic Garden—afforded him a different experience altogether, and the opportunity to see and learn about exotic plants. After leaving the British Isles, Shaw proceeded across Europe to Egypt and on to Russia, then to Stockholm and Copenhagen. Throughout the trip he stayed in contact with his sister Caroline and the caretaker of his new country property, Bernard O'Halloran, and seemed satisfied to let business proceed without him. He would receive notice of his father's impending death in late April 1844 (Joseph Shaw was buried at Mount Hope in Rochester, New York) but would not return to console his family. Shaw was busy enjoying himself. In letters his cousin teased him about the "Continental loves" he had acquired, in particular a French acquaintance, Aimée Dupont. In her letters to Shaw after his return, she sent kisses and told of trembling at the thought of him.

When Shaw returned from this second Grand Tour in August 1846 and checked into his suite at the Planters' House Hotel, St. Louis was in the midst of its most vital decade of growth.[19] In size and productivity, the city eclipsed those around it, including the oldest permanent settlement in Missouri, Ste. Genevieve, the French Creole town to the south that competed with St. Louis as a trade center. Shaw's business continued to prosper: his downtown property now included an assortment of lots on Front Street facing the river, many prime corner lots downtown, and entire blocks.[20] His circle of associates was also growing. He continued to deal with the city's most prestigious entrepreneurs—Charles P. Chouteau, L. A. Benoist, and John O'Fallon—and was also becoming acquainted with citizens who contributed to the fields of education, science, and medicine. One of these figures was the German emigrant George Engelmann, a general practitioner and obstetrician who happened to have a passion for botany.

The civic progress of St. Louis was forestalled in 1849 by a cholera epidemic that took nearly four thousand lives, and then by the devastating Great Fire of May 17. Ignited by sparks from the steamboat *White Cloud*, lighting two dozen other steamers loaded with combustible goods such as tobacco and cotton, the fire spread quickly. Warehouses and offices along the levee and buildings that housed the city's vital businesses were destroyed, including the newspaper presses of the *Republican* and the *Telegraph*, the United States Hotel, and countless other buildings constituting the core of downtown. The fire irrevocably altered the waterfront and commercial center (yet damaged none of Shaw's property) and prompted massive rebuilding and reorganization. Streets were widened, and lost landmarks were replaced by substantial blocks of stores and business palaces. With the rebuilding, the city recovered; refined businesses, such as the jewelers, daguerreotype galleries, and milliners on Fourth Street, considered the Broadway of St. Louis, complemented new foundries, sawmills, and machine shops. Newly built hotels also reflected the sophisticated nature of a city that had now grown to nearly 77,000 residents. The Lindell Hotel, owned by Shaw associates Peter and Jesse Lindell, and designed by the local architect George I. Barnett, graciously welcomed visitors traveling the frontier.

It was the new Planters' House Hotel, where Shaw resided, that was the most representative of life in this increasingly cosmopolitan city. With an air of "wealth, fashion, adventure, ease, romance—all the dreams of the new life in the great West,"[21] it rivaled counterparts such as the Astor House in New York City (Shaw had stayed at the Astor, and was in a position to compare the two firsthand). Charles Dickens and his wife had stayed at the Planters' during their six-month tour of America and commended its creature comforts and the bounty of dishes served at dinner. (Dickens's complimentary description of the hotel experience stood in contrast to his description of the Mississippi River, which he referred to as an enormous ditch of liquid mud.) It is not surprising that Shaw chose to live at the Planters' in between his periods of travel to England and the Continent. To a well-traveled (and single) gentleman, who had stayed in the finest hotels in Europe, the downtown landmark that had been described

"An Open and Undulating Half Prairie, Half Shrubbery"

as the "universal *rendezvous* for the Mississippi Valley"[22] was an appropriate temporary home base.

But most successful merchants and professionals, especially those with families, did not consider hotels "home." A few very wealthy families began to build country estates, such as the Chambers family's Taille de Noyer, Major Richard Graham's Hazelwood, and the Bissell family's country place,[23] but the majority of the city's affluent citizens moved into the comfortable and impressive neighborhoods that were springing up just outside the central business district. Besides fine houses and neighborhoods, they wanted gardens and parks, for their beauty and as markers of refined living. The residents of exclusive Lucas Place, for example, enjoyed the landscaped squares of Washington Park and Missouri Park. The thirty-acre Lafayette Park provided a complement to the elegant Second Empire, Federal, and Romanesque residences of the Lafayette Square neighborhood that surrounded it.[24] Farther west, the high ground near the intersection of Lafayette and Grand Avenues was becoming a fashionable address, and in 1848 Shaw devised a plan for landscaping its southwest corner lot.[25] He labeled it a "park garden," and included an arboretum, pinetum, and rock works similar to those at Chatsworth. Its impressive collection of florists' flowers, roses, and weeping, variegated, and native trees was to be organized using the botanical classifications of Jussieu and Linnaeus (the garden would even have a curator's house and museum). Shaw's plan, though never implemented, reveals his idea of what fashionable residential grounds should include and served as a precursor to plans he would consider on a vast scale the following year at his country property.

Ready to have his own residence and grounds, Shaw commissioned George I. Barnett to build a town house and country villa for him in 1849. Like Shaw, Barnett had been born in England; he was from Nottingham, not too far from Sheffield, and had come to the United States ten years before, at the age of twenty-four. Barnett admired the work of the English Baroque architect

OPPOSITE: *Shaw's plan for a "park garden" at the corner of Lafayette and Grand Avenues, ca. 1848.*

Christopher Wren, and understood the idea that architectural style should be appropriate to function and location. He designed Shaw's projects accordingly. The town house was formal, suited to city life and entertaining business associates, and was the proper kind of residence for a man of Shaw's wealth and standing in the community. Located at the southwest corner of Seventh and Locust Streets, it had seventeen rooms and two kitchens (but no space for a garden), and was classical in form. Its cubic shape, symmetrical facade, and refined ornament made reference to the homes of wealthy and powerful Florentine families of the Italian Renaissance such as the Medici (the style had been appropriated in England by architect Inigo Jones). Inside, it was decorated with English tiles from Stoke-on-Trent, Brussels carpets, and marble mantels from New York. In size, it was easily large enough for Shaw, his sisters, and his mother to live in, or for a wife and family, but Henry lived there alone except for domestic help.

In contrast to the town house, Barnett designed Shaw's country "villa" in the Italianate mode, a fashionable style at midcentury and very different from the classical look of his town house.

Tower Grove House in 1890.

The Italianate style took traditional forms and rearranged them with picturesque irregularity, using various shapes and sizes of windows and a mix of colors and textures, and always included an asymmetrical tower as part of the design. Arbiters of taste believed that the style was perfectly suited to the countryside and reflected the informality of country living. Perhaps it is only by coincidence that Shaw's villa bore a striking resemblance to Joseph Paxton's house, Barbrook, at Chatsworth, where early experiments in gardening had taken place. Barnett situated the house facing north, toward the original grove of trees on the site. From the top of the tower one could look out over the fields and survey work being done below (and someday, over gardens); on the south an arched loggia, or porch, overlooked the back of the property.

Soon after Barnett had been commissioned, construction on the house began and Shaw ordered plants. One can imagine Shaw and his architect on the site, supervising work and sorting out possibilities for the arrangement of the garden. The number and variety of plants he ordered were staggering, and he would spend two years filling the acres of beds to his satisfaction. Local and midwestern suppliers filled the earliest orders: Nicholas Riehl, just south in Gravois, and John Thorburn sent orders in the fall and spring of 1849–50; orders from Cincinnati's Clifton Nursery date to 1850 and the following spring. These four orders, along with other supplemental ones, transformed the fields around Shaw's villa. Besides providing plants, some suppliers suggested placement, offered to provide labor, and sent advice tailored to the midwestern climate—a valuable service at a time when propagation information specific to one's region was difficult to obtain. In one case, the *Western Horticultural Review*, written by Dr. Warder, was suggested as a guide; other early but more general guides Shaw used were Bernard MacMahon's *American Gardener's Calendar* and Hovey's *Magazine of Horticulture*. Trees and shrubs were planted first, providing a framework for the garden; then Shaw added roses—one of his favorites—and perennials, and lastly, brilliant-colored exotics for bedding out, borders, and in decorative urns.

Thorburn's October 1849 order included fifty-eight shrubs—white, pink, and "deep, dark pink" flowering spirea, and yellow, variegated, and scarlet (or coral) sweet honeysuckle; and Shaw's notes indicate their placement near trees and specifically near his "pink pea blossomed rose acacia."[26] Fifty mixed garden roses were to be planted eight feet apart, two feet from the fence, in good, rich soil, for a charge of ten dollars. Providing Shaw an example of his work, Thorburn dug up the end of the border by the garden gate, pointing out the improvements that would result to the "Arboreum [*sic*] ring"—possibly a reference to rows of concentric plantings in the arboretum. The next April, Nicholas Riehl sent him fruit and nut trees (dwarf apple, pear, filberts), ornamental trees and shrubs (white mulberry, a double almond, white lilac), grapevines, and one hundred *Iris pumila*. Roses arrived in the dozens: hardy roses, moss roses (loved by Victorians for their "cozy" quality), climbers, and a General DuBourg. The order was completed by shipment of a double tree peony, robinias, fourteen more assorted roses, and another two thousand iris. A huge order of specimen plants and trees arrived in May 1850 from Clifton, and Shaw used the one thousand *Maclura pomifera* from the order, better known as Osage orange or hedge apple trees, to line his private drive. He received a fair return on his investment of ten dollars—several remain stately today.[27]

The plants that Shaw chose were a mix of native and "exotic" types—those indigenous to other regions, and often other conti-

Osage oranges along Shaw's private entry drive.

Photo by Carol Betsch.

View in the grove with specimen Amur cork tree in background.
Photo by Carol Betsch.

nents—many of which had to be cared for as annuals or wintered over in plant houses. Clifton Nursery claimed to have the largest stock of hardy trees and plants in the Midwest and, for practical reasons understood by horticulturists, encouraged the use of native plants. But the company had yielded to the popular interest in showy specimens from other parts of the world, and supplied their customers with a wide range of exotic plants as well. They commented that their inventory of exotics would always be "anx-

"An Open and Undulating Half Prairie, Half Shrubbery"

illary [*sic*] to our large collection of hardy plants," suggesting both a demand for unusual specimens and a sensitivity to what was becoming a debate about plant choice and propriety.

Critics condemned the use of nonindigenous plants for a variety of reasons ranging from the practical to the esoteric. They claimed that nonnative plants were inappropriate in American gardens and that their use implied a reference to art (and artifice) rather than nature. Writers such as Thoreau spoke of the reverence, purity, and truth of nature; the cultivation of native plants was one manifestation of this belief. A. J. Downing acknowledged that native plants were preferable because they were hardy; many critics believed that plants from jungles and deserts appeared gaudy and failed to harmonize with, or adapt to, the North American context. According to this school of thought, the dramatic size and showy patterns of exotic specimens constituted a "museum of costly curiosities."[28] What had begun as a question of plant choice evolved into a debate with political and moral overtones, with critics chastising exotics for being fake, foreign, and un-American. In the twentieth century their use would even be considered "effeminate."[29] Despite protests, and even as the century drew to a close, popular and professional opinion was split on the strict use of native plants and the use of exotics. As late as 1875 nurseryman and horticulturalist Peter Henderson, in *Gardening for Pleasure*, wrote of the delightful contrast and interest created by beds massed with cannas, salvia, *Alternanthera*, and lobelia. Prominent landscape advocates including Frederick Law Olmsted, Warren Manning, and even Jens Jensen occasionally relied on nonnative plants to add variety to their designs.

Shaw approved of the use of exotic plants not only for the interest and variety they added to the garden but as the symbolic reward for a century of scientific discovery. Just as plant hunters of the eighteenth century had brought species from other continents and introduced them to England, Shaw saw the virtue in bringing the rare and unusual plants he appreciated to his country estate. Such an act would become a way to educate people about botany,

Decorative lath house and caladium bedding, Missouri Botanical Garden, 1908.

to cultivate taste, and to improve the standard of living by creating a refined environment. That such plants could be costly indulgences, and novelties, was part of their appeal. He viewed exotic plants in the same way that connoisseurs viewed works of art: they should be valued for their intrinsic beauty and unique characteristics, and be collected and cared for because of these qualities.

Shaw was not alone in terms of taste or in his interest in creating collections of exotic plants. Other wealthy Americans were fervently collecting exotics for their estates. At exactly the same time, at his home in the Hudson Valley, Wodenethe, Henry Winthrop Sargent was buying up exotic plants from nurseries all over America and Europe,[30] planting a huge assortment of foreign trees and shrubs. Critics claimed Sargent's interest was in horticultural oddities and freaks, but like Shaw he was intrigued by the variety in nature—especially weeping, cutleaf, dwarf, and variegated forms of conifers and trees—and he built a collection that was not unlike a collection of art. Shaw acquired a similar

Date palm exhibited as a work of art at Shaw's garden, 1890.

mix of exotics, including the bold *Araucaria imbricata* (similar to the Victorian favorite, the monkey puzzle tree) and *Cedrus deodara* (deodar), which were sent with directions for helping them winter over. He also ordered pelargoniums, fuchsia, oleander, and antirrhinum, along with camellias, chrysanthemums, and picotee carnations. These flowers would be cultivated successfully in Shaw's plant houses, but ultimately his experience with many exotic trees, which failed not only to flourish but even to survive, forced him to admit they were a poor choice for Missouri.

By the fall of 1849, Shaw was occupying the Tower Grove house from time to time, and the gardening continued. He oversaw such necessities and improvements as mowing, the building of fences, the construction of tree tubs and screens (possibly as protection against animals), and the construction of a beehive, which took six days to complete. In December, just in time for winter, Shaw contracted for the building of a plant house to protect his newest exotic specimens—and possibly to cultivate the picotee carnations he had ordered. Its glass, putty, white lead, and gilded vane cost him $23.70. Spring planting in 1851 embellished what he had already in place: more pines, spruce, and mahonias came from Clifton Nursery, whose owner insisted he had a great many more things Shaw needed. One hundred fifty celery and two hundred cabbage plants were bought locally, as were, again from Nicholas Riehl, black Hamburg grapes, poplars, and weeping willows. More shrubs were needed for effect—four varieties of *Philadelphus* (mock orange) and spirea, syringa, and *Lonicera* (honeysuckle). Another large lot of roses arrived—moss rose, Princesse Marie, Triomphe des Bourbons—"to be planted in pots" depending on the severity of cold weather. Dahlias, primula, and *Aconitum japonicum* (monkshood) all heightened the seasonal show in the garden beds; *Passiflora* (passionflower) vines and the beanlike seeds of catalpa trees added variety; anemones sprang from his "showy border." In November, cherry trees, Norway spruce, and euonymus arrived from Ellwanger and Barry's Mount Hope Nursery in Rochester, New York.

Both of Shaw's sisters shared an interest in plants. Sarah longed to see the wildflowers scattered across the prairie, and she wrote her brother of her wish to cultivate rare flowers in her Rochester garden. Caroline shared his knowledge of plants and recorded the organization of his plantings in her garden journal. Their interest in the subject reflects the widespread popularity of botany-related hobbies—searching the countryside for native plants ("botanizing") and the more genteel act of cultivating one's own garden. People of middle and upper income, and of moderate and higher education, were drawn to this new field of interest, and gardening was suitable for both sexes—it was considered not only proper but a morally correct activity for women. Gardening was facilitated by new techniques and instruments, such as insecticidal dusting machines, novelty watering pots, and the lawn mower; by new means of construction and new materials such as iron and affordable glass for greenhouses; and by the new field of horticultural journalism, which educated the middle-class audience on methods and provided information about new varieties. Besides being interesting and fulfilling, garden botany was also a sign of status. In an age that valued improvement and innovation, it was a comment on one's taste and education. Gardening (and plant collecting) was also about ownership: the length of one's plant list reflected the size of one's bank account; the scale of one's greenhouse—from lean-to to huge conservatory—said the same.

Sister Caroline's 1851 journal inventory of the grounds at Tower Grove House, probably begun in the late spring and maintained over the summer months in her brother's absence, indicates the scope of Shaw's investment in gardening and documents the extensive collection begun only two years before. Her thirty-six pages, fourteen of which cover the arboretum portion of the garden, suggest both the range and diversity of Shaw's plantings from 1849 to 1851. Her inventory is organized by specific location, clearly indicating each border and bed—"main or middle border in the Garden," for instance, or "2nd division of the East Border beginning at the North end"—and by plant type, with separate categories for the bulbs, evergreens, annuals, and greenhouse plants (in pots) in the arboretum. A heavily planted red and white border lined the arboretum: red roses, white lilies, hydrangeas, white lilac, and snowberry bush were planted along the drive. Another portion of the border was filled with unusual combinations such as roses and raspberries placed next to each other. Herbaceous beds of flax, peony, clematis, and iris were juxtaposed with beds of sunflowers, mignonette, and celosia, used as annuals in Missouri's seasonally harsh climate. Some of the exotics from the 1850 Clifton Nursery and Nicholas Riehl orders were exhibited in pots and tubs (perhaps part of Shaw's large order from the famous foundry at Coalbrookdale, England) and wintered over in the greenhouse. Caroline indicates plants brought or sent from Rochester, suggesting they were either gifts from their property or from the Mount Hope or Genesee Falls nurseries there.

Caroline's journal, which records Shaw's first private gardens and the major planting he undertook, also provides insight into planting practices and taste at midcentury. The riot of color, texture, and variety in the garden anticipate the multipatterned and highly decorated interiors gaining popularity, but Shaw held the extravagant composition in check in two ways. First, to give a sense of order to the design he arranged plants by type—a reference to botanical systems of classification. Rather than use historical models such as Tudor or Elizabethan revival styles which were a decorative means of organization, he chose an approach based on science and more indicative of current taste. Second, he employed color theory to make the visual impression of the garden beds as harmonious as possible. For example, Shaw's plant choices and their arrangement in the arboretum's red and white border suggest the current interest in the role of complementary colors and human perception as they apply to flower placement. Some theorists believed that using red in peripheral rather than central beds helped increase the apparent size of the display. Likewise, red flowers should be planted alongside white to increase the harmonious effect against the background of green—red's complementary color—provided by the surrounding leaves and lawn.[31]

Before Shaw left on his third and final trip abroad in June 1851, though he would only be gone seven months, he drew up his first will assigning money, personal items, and property to relatives, employees, and slaves in the event of his death. He set aside money for his burial at Bellefontaine Cemetery and gave his brother-in-law Julius Morisse—Caroline's new husband—power of attorney. Much of this tour was spent in Britain visiting a variety of landscapes, from Liverpool to the rocky and picturesque terrain around the village of Matlock and the cascades of the river Derwent and its gorge nearby. He stopped at the estate of Chatsworth, then continued on through Derbyshire and Devonshire, through Wales, and on to the verdant greensward of Hyde Park in London.

Shaw stayed in London from August 3 through August 15 to visit the Great Exhibition of the Works of Industry of All Nations, planned in part by Queen Victoria's husband, Prince Albert, which had opened May 1. "The world" was heading to the exhibition by railroad and on horseback, from nearby counties and from the other side of the Atlantic Ocean. Six million people, ultimately, would attend. Henry's uncle James Hoole confirmed that it was the main occupation of their attention and not to be missed. Those who visited celebrated Britain's position as the most powerful and productive empire in history, and Queen Victoria described it as the nation's greatest day. This first world's fair brought together arts, crafts, and manufactures from around the globe. Nations exhibited machinery, fine art, and handmade wares to a public eager for a taste of the exotic and inventive. Of the thousands of exhibits, Shaw was no doubt eager to see that of his cousin's firm, H. Hoole and Company, Sheffield, a lacquered brass fire surround designed by the notable sculptor Alfred G. Stevens, chief designer for the company between 1850 and 1857, whose designs were also produced at the well-known foundry at Coalbrookdale.[32]

The highlight of the visit for Shaw, however, was not the exhibition's collections or his cousin's entry. It was the building that housed them, dubbed the "Crystal Palace" in a newspaper account: Joseph Paxton's skeletal frame of glass and iron that had been inspired by the structural form of the underside of a lily pad. The building's iron bracing clad with glass mimicked the strong yet delicate veining, hidden beneath the water's surface, that enables tropical lilies to float. The Crystal Palace was a variation of the water lily house Paxton had designed and built at Chatsworth a decade earlier, which constituted a giant improvement in conservatory design and operation. Its innovative materials and construction, snapped together on-site by laborers and removed at the end of the exhibition, were the antithesis of conventional architecture—monuments built by craftsmen from traditional materials, meant to last generations—and made the exhibition hall itself a statement of English innovation. It was Joseph Paxton's

work, his "palace" and his ongoing projects at Chatsworth, that lit Shaw's imagination. Visiting Chatsworth just before his arrival in London, he was able to discuss plants and gardening with the estate's head and junior gardeners, and he had seen the culmination of Paxton's work: the first Victoria water lily to bloom in England was growing there, the arboretum was flourishing, and the conservatories had been recently completed.

Shaw considered the achievements of Paxton and William Spencer Cavendish, the sixth duke of Devonshire, and made a major decision. St. Louis—America—deserved a garden that would showcase garden botany in the same way that Chatsworth shared its beauty and botanical innovation. Why couldn't the success, and delight, he had experienced creating his private garden at Tower Grove be shared with the public? When he arrived home in December, he would apply all his interest in horticulture and botany and begin planning a much larger project, a public botanical garden at his country estate.

"Kew in Miniature"

THE FOUNDING OF SHAW'S GARDEN

For all classes of society a garden may be considered an object of interest, of instruction, and amusement. . . . Horticulture and botanical science will thus contribute to the promotion of pure taste and pleasant recreation.

—HENRY SHAW, *Guide to the Missouri Botanical Garden* (ca. 1870)

In the summer of 1853 Henry Shaw stopped in the office of a business associate, the St. Louis real estate agent Richard Smith Elliott. With a bouquet of flowers in his hand, he looked at a map of the city and told Elliott about his plan to create a botanical garden, complete with "proper accessories," free and open to citizens and strangers alike.[1] The visit to Chatsworth two years before had validated and brought into focus what he had been contemplating for a decade. Strolling through the arboretum there, and past conservatories that sheltered orchids and blooming water lilies, he had asked himself why he, too, could not create such a place. With the help of slaves and Irish immigrants it had taken him three

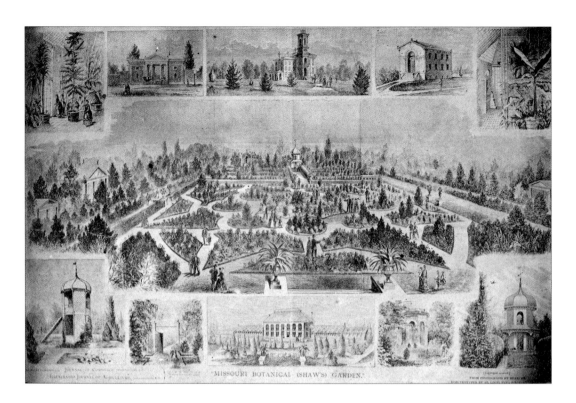

"MISSOURI BOTANICAL (SHAW'S) GARDEN."

Drawing of Shaw's Garden with vignettes. From Illustrated Journal of Agriculture, *ca. 1880.*

years to transform the rolling prairie and waving grasses of the countryside into his impressive private collection of gardens at Tower Grove. Shaw knew that a public botanical garden would take greater planning and more time to implement; sharing the news of his intention with Elliott was a clear indication that he had begun.

The January before, Shaw had embarked on what would be a five-year period of study and planning. In his "Notes on Vegetation" he began by carefully recording plant habit and growth, barometric pressure, temperature, rainfall, and cloudiness. He wrote of gathering "George IV" peaches in September of that year (Paxton, at Chatsworth, had gathered a record bounty of peaches from its "Royal George" tree—the finest in Britain—exactly a decade before). He recorded fact and observation: the size of fruit as it developed (peaches the size of filberts, Black Hamburg grapes the size of peas), when plants began to bud and blossom, the date temperatures were increased in the vinery; he recorded harvesting the first bowl of strawberries from the garden and noted the last day in August there were violets. The notes refer to a number of different buildings for the growth and propagation of plants—hothouses, vineries, a new plant house—the construction of which he had overseen since the completion of his house.

Shaw had also put together an impressive collection of books on the subject of landscape and horticulture as resources for study. In 1854 the shelves at Tower Grove included Humphry Repton's writings on landscape gardening, Joseph Paxton's *Botanical Dictionary*, a five-volume set of the *British Florist*, A. J. Downing's *Fruit and Fruit Trees of America*, and five different works by John Claudius Loudon, including his *Encyclopedia of Architecture*, *Encyclopedia of Gardening*, *The Suburban Gardener*, and the eight-volume *Arboretum and Fruticetum Britannicum*.[2] Two works on botany for women, one by Jane Webb (Mrs. John Claudius) Loudon and another by John Lindley, were on his shelves, as were general references on botany, including one by Priscilla Bell Wakefield and another by John Hutton Balfour, along with works addressing specific subjects including the propagation of carnations, beekeeping, and farm and stable economy.[3] Between trips to the vinery and plant houses, Shaw pored over these works, educating himself on all aspects of the subject relevant to a botanical garden. He admitted to an "immensity of labour, *wearing out my eyes and cudgeling my brains*" in search of information.[4]

For Shaw the idea of Chatsworth persisted, especially the monumental conservatories and the world-class botanical collection there. The productive partnership of Joseph Paxton and William Spencer Cavendish, which had begun in 1826, resulted in additions to Chatsworth that were fashionable and imitated.[5] The duke, "bit by gardening" and aided by the luxury of unlimited resources, had proceeded to create a botanical garden and collection like no other. The arboretum Paxton planted in 1835 was a museum-worthy collection of native and exotic trees and shrubs. He had responded to his employer's passion for orchids, water lilies, and camellias by experimentation with and construction of over twenty plant houses to accommodate the estate's growing collection of finds from plant-hunting expeditions to

India, South America, and other far-off locales. The Great Conservatory (1840), Conservative wall (1842), Vinery (1848), and Lily House (1850, for the duke's *Victoria* water lily) were Paxton's inventive solutions to the problem of housing tropical and nonnative specimens. This remarkable collection of both plants and buildings so impressed Shaw that he hoped to emulate them.

But there was another aspect of Chatsworth which particularly appealed to Shaw, and that was its accessibility to the general public, who were welcomed free of charge.[6] By the mid-nineteenth century Chatsworth was hosting huge numbers of day-trippers who left cities and crossed counties to see the garden and park. In the summer of 1849, when extension of the railroad had expedited the trip, nearly 80,000 people came. These visitors were not only granted access to the grounds, they were practically catered to: "The humblest individual is not only shown the whole but the Duke has expressly ordered the waterworks [the Emperor Fountain] to be played for everyone without exception."[7] Chatsworth impressed not only those unaccustomed to such spectacular surroundings, but even visitors jaded by luxury and learning; Queen Victoria and Prince Albert invited themselves on short notice, and Charles Darwin was transported with delight by the cultivation of nature there. These were the aspects of Chatsworth which Shaw hoped to replicate: a place open to all, with a botanical collection so arranged that it inspired and entertained everyone who came, from the youngest to the most seasoned visitor.

But Shaw realized that there were aspects of the English aristocratic estate that made it an inappropriate model for an American institution. Bess Hardwick had first cultivated the Chatsworth property when she planted herbs and dug fishponds in 1560; it had served a single aristocratic family for nearly three centuries, and had been designed, and redesigned, by the foremost figures in English landscape, including William Kent and "Capability" Brown. Shaw, on the other hand, was an amateur advocate of landscape, and the property he planned to shape was a remnant of communal fields, farms, and open pasture that lay just west of the Mississippi River. Created by a single individual, his garden would be a cultural and educational institution made to serve a public of middle-class citizens. Shaw realized the need for practical models that had a more limited size and budget.[8]

One such model was the eight-acre garden in Glasgow, Scotland, for its size and for the improvements made under William Jackson Hooker's tenure there. Hooker's catalogue of plants at Glasgow, published in 1825, included a plan and alphabetical list of specimens which could be used as a reference. In 1841, Hooker had gone on to become the director of the Royal Botanic Gardens at Kew, establishing its economic botany collections and overseeing the building of the great Palm House there in 1844–48. (Shaw knew better, of course, than to hope to replicate Kew's vast collection, although the Palm House could serve as a model). Another model was the botanical garden at Liverpool, which housed an important collection and was considered an outstanding public "garden of instruction" in spite of its small size of five acres. The eighteen-acre garden in Shaw's hometown of Sheffield was one more example to consider; it had been praised as a "model" botanical garden and written up in *Gardener's Magazine* in 1839.[9] Established on farmland purchased in 1834, it was created to provide recreation and education to Sheffield's residents and as a response to growing concerns about

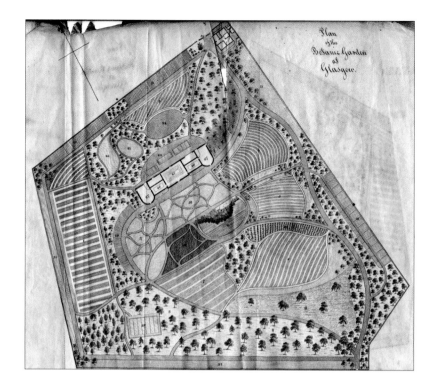

Plan of the Botanic Garden at Glasgow, in Henry Shaw's collection.

the lack of open green space for public use. From the beginning, Robert Marnock, the head gardener, horticulturist, and first curator of gardens in 1836, directed the improvement of the grounds. Shaw's return visits to Sheffield permitted him to view progress there, and to see how its fruticetum and arboretum, like those at Chatsworth, provided convenient means of organizing trees and shrubs by type. As Shaw considered the organization of his own plantings, he also thought about architecture and accessories for the garden—the Ionic-style main gate (1836) and glass conservatories at Sheffield were appropriate and handsome, and had caught his eye.

The Sheffield garden was also one of the first examples of the newly popular gardenesque plantings, defined by Loudon in 1832, that Shaw would have seen too. First fashionable in England, and later in America, the gardenesque approach was characterized by scattered plantings that allowed trees and plants to be viewed as specimens, observed in the round, almost like sculp-

ture. The application of such an approach in a botanical garden was logical—education and observation were primary concerns, and the ability to view the characteristics of plants, especially those that had been transported from the far corners of the world, facilitated learning. Seeing Marnock's use of the gardenesque method at Sheffield confirmed, in Shaw's mind, the propriety of its use for such purposes. That Loudon commended Marnock's excellent taste in landscape gardening would have encouraged Shaw as well.[10]

As Shaw thought about the specifications of these botanical gardens, and read and sorted ideas for his own, he continued to record notes on vegetation and make improvements at his private garden at Tower Grove. In 1855 there was a final rush of activity on the grounds surrounding the house: he had George Barnett design an arbor for the property, and a team of workers constructed another vinery.[11] He bought new tools—pruning shears and budding knife—vegetable and flower seeds, and a copy of *Barry's Fruit Garden* for $1.25. In November, he received another huge assortment of plants from Robert Buist in Philadelphia: exotics, roses (hybrid perpetuals, bourbon, damask, china, and tea roses), more grapevines, nectarines, and pears; showy bulbs such

The main conservatory at the Sheffield Botanic Garden, 1850. From Catalogue, Descriptive and Historical, of the Rare and Interesting Plants [at Sheffield Botanic Garden] *(ca. 1850).*

as amaryllis, crown imperial fritillaria, and lilies. Landscape gardening had become Shaw's main pursuit—planning, organizing garden spaces, overseeing the construction of plant houses, horticulture; it claimed much of his time. It is unclear exactly when he learned that little more than three miles away a fellow St. Louisan, a physician named George Engelmann, was equally enthralled by plants and had the capacity to give Shaw important assistance. For Dr. Engelmann, it was the science of plants—botany—that provided the greatest satisfaction.

George Engelmann and Botanical Discovery in the West

George Engelmann (1809–84) arrived in the Midwest in 1832.[12] He was twenty-three, with a degree in medicine when he came to North America as an advance agent for German relatives pursuing frontier investments. Born in Frankfurt-am-Main, Engelmann had studied theology at Heidelberg, Berlin, and Würzburg, where he received a doctorate in medicine in 1831. After a period of study in Paris alongside Louis Agassiz and Alexander Braun (who would become, respectively, an important naturalist and a noted botanist), Engelmann emigrated to North America, where he lived briefly at a German settlement in Belleville, Illinois. Once in St. Louis, in 1833, he set up practice as an obstetrician and general practitioner, and his success was brought in part by his fluency in English, German, and French.[13] From his arrival he was a keen observer of natural phenomena, recording the first systematic data of the area's mineral deposits, animals, and temperature. The Midwest was the ideal location for the young doctor to nourish his passion for the natural sciences, which he eagerly engaged in in his first years there. In 1835 he set out on horseback to collect and record local minerals and plants in the Meramec River valley, an area rich in specimens. Two years later, he explored the region to the south, in Arkansas,

George Engelmann.

with the same mission. As a novice field naturalist, he made observations and drawings of the prairie, mines, and hot springs,
and he collected and dried plant specimens.

Engelmann's primary interest, which he discovered during his
training as a physician, was in the science of plants. Because plants
were the source of most medicine before the twentieth century, he
had been taught botany in medical school, and his extremely
sophisticated background in the subject is reflected in his first
scientific publication, which dealt with abnormal plant forms.[14]
Engelmann's eagerness to study in a region full of virtually undis-
covered plants was apparent from his arrival in the Midwest, and
he jumped at the opportunity to identify and record plants that
had yet to be designated with Latin names, and thus make contributions to a field that was in its infancy. Although doctoring provided the funds to engage in his true passion, it left him little time
to do so, and the plant hunting and field trips he indulged in on
his arrival were soon limited by his growing medical practice.

During the 1840s and early 1850s Engelmann was able to remain involved with botany by balancing long hours of delivering babies and dealing with seasonal cholera epidemics and scarlet fever with his new role as a facilitator for plant-finding expeditions. St. Louis had become the jumping-off point for traders and explorers and was gaining a reputation as the "Gateway to the West." The discovery, identification, and collection of plants in western and southwestern North America was vastly increasing the body of botanical knowledge, and plant hunters used the city as their hub. Engelmann organized more than thirty westward expeditions into newly opened territories—recruiting, outfitting, and serving as adviser—with the chance to document findings and participate in plant distribution and sale.[15]

Plant hunters sent roots, seeds, and living plants back to Engelmann in St. Louis. Sets of specimens were bundled for transport, reinforced with splints of wood or reeds, and bound with twine made from leaves of agave or another sinuous plant material.[16] Plants were first dried, then mounted, labeled, and organized into notebooks or collections called herbaria, and used for scientific study. Several collectors Engelmann worked with had been acquaintances in Germany and had been enticed by the prospect of new collecting opportunities: Ferdinand Lindheimer, whom Engelmann had known in Frankfurt, collected plants on his behalf in Texas, and Friedrich Adolph Wislizenus, also trained as a physician (he ultimately became Engelmann's medical partner and oversaw the practice when Engelmann was absent for fieldwork), traveled as far as Panama in his searches. Karl Andreas Geyer, a former gardener from Dresden who gained expertise traveling with the explorer John Frémont and who gathered plants in the northern United States, and Augustus Fendler, who went to Santa Fe to "ravish" the rich territory of the southern Rocky Mountains (who would serve for a short time as the botanical garden's curator), both had working relationships with Engelmann.[17] Thomas Nuttall, a preeminent British botanist who completed three major trips west of the Mississippi River and published (among other works) a catalog on North American plants known up to 1817, communicated with Engelmann about plants coming from Sante Fe, via other plant hunters. Late at night, when Engelmann had finished with patients for the day, he would unpack specimens, make careful observations, and then record their characteristics in definitive monographs.

The discipline and rigor of German scientific investigation that Engelmann contributed to American botany, and by extension, to the discovery of the West,[18] resulted in the identification of more than six hundred species new to science.[19] Charles Sprague Sargent, the founding director of the Arnold Arboretum of Harvard University, noted Engelmann's scientific acumen, which was applied in long monographs on a number of different plant groups including American oaks, conifers, and euphorbias.[20] Besides the Meramec River area and Arkansas, he studied in the Missouri Ozarks, Illinois, the Appalachian Mountains, Louisiana, and farther afield in the Lake Superior region, on the Pacific coast, in southern Arizona, and in the Rocky Mountains. Considered by many to be the foremost authority on cacti, he wrote authoritative studies on the giant saguaro cactus (including his contribution to the 1859 *Cactaceae of the Boundary*), and on oak trees, ferns, and grapes; many of his findings remain fundamental to the field. His interest in viticulture resulted in the discovery of a remedy for the phylloxera epidemic, a parasitic disease of the vine attributed to the plant louse, which affected European vineyards.[21] Instrumental in the formation of the first scientific institution west of the Alleghenies, the Academy of Science of St. Louis,[22] he is commemorated by numerous species including *Ophioglossum engelmannii* Prantl and the genus *Engelmannia* Torr. & A. Gray.[23] Engelmann's personal herbarium grew to 97,000 specimens,[24] and his fieldwork resulted in sixty volumes of drawings and notes on frontier plant life.[25]

Engelmann established close working relationships with botanists in the East, including John Torrey (1796–1873) and Asa Gray (1810–88),[26] who, along with Engelmann, were considered

to be the foremost authorities on North American plants at mid-century.[27] As Torrey and Gray collaborated on the revolutionary work that was the basis of their *Flora of North America*,[28] Engelmann and Gray began a partnership based on shared interests and contributions to the field: both were founding members of scientific organizations (the National Academy of Sciences, and Gray of the Academy of Science of St. Louis as well), and they counted leading thinkers of the day as friends and colleagues (both knew Charles Darwin, who had confided his theory of evolution to Gray as he developed it).[29] While in England, Gray met with the botanists John Lindley, Robert Brown, William Jackson Hooker, and his son and successor Joseph Dalton Hooker; Engelmann visited with Alexander von Humboldt when in Berlin and with William Hooker when at Kew. But the greatest bond for Engelmann and Gray was their shared passion for North American plants, particularly the many species in the West that had not yet been discovered.

When Engelmann returned from his wedding trip to Germany in 1840, he stopped in New York to meet with Asa Gray. From this first meeting, the two were bound by their joint mission of botanical investigation. By 1851 their collaboration had resulted in four important plant-finding expeditions, to Texas, New Mexico, northern Mexico, and the southern Rocky Mountains. Engelmann's role as organizer and adviser was complemented by Gray and his eastern access to scientific publications and herbaria. The two divided the labor of collecting, sorting, documenting, publication, and sale of specimens.[30] Engelmann

Asa Gray.

depended on his medical practice to finance his botanical activity, but Gray was the first American to earn his living at botany, until then a subdiscipline of medicine. Appointed the Fisher Professor of Natural Sciences at Harvard in 1842, he taught students and took charge of a seven-acre botanical garden, which he hoped to fill with little-known plants from the West. Engelmann helped make Gray's wish possible by obtaining cacti, agaves, and yuccas from the area Gray considered to be the most interesting region in North America—the Rocky Mountains and land to the south. This area was rich but unexplored; Linnaeus knew of only one species of cactus from the area that is now the United States, and Nuttall added a few more, but Engelmann's work increased the number to more than one hundred.[31]

By the 1850s circumstances began to change for George Engelmann, after early days when his study of botany was secondary. He had once admitted to Gray that he had "neither the leisure, nor books, collections, etc. sufficient to do the work alone, nor do it so well as to be credible," but since then the situation had improved.[32] In 1856, as the two planned to work together at the Harvard Botanic Garden and Gray's Herbarium in Cambridge that summer, Engelmann was presented with a new opportunity, one that would allow him the chance to study and travel even farther in pursuit of botany. In April he wrote to Gray about the St. Louis resident and bachelor he had recently met, the "very rich Englishman," Henry Shaw, who had decided to spend his time and money founding a botanical garden and collection, "Kew in miniature."[33] This meeting, which would lead to decades of collaboration and friendship, was catalyzed by William Jackson Hooker (1785–1865), the director of the Royal Botanic Garden at Kew, considered by many to be the dean of world botany. Hooker had suggested that Shaw, who had written to him for advice, contact Dr. Engelmann, who, as a world-class yet local botanical expert, could provide him with guidance.[34] Engelmann saw the opportunity to further the state of botany in the Midwest by persuading Shaw to create a serious research institution complete with a herbarium and library—resources that would draw experts from all over the world. Likewise, Asa Gray applauded the project's potential and Shaw's unique garden of western plants; there was no botanical garden in America open to the public at the time, and Shaw's contribution would facilitate learning for the public and scientists alike.

Shaw had first written to William Hooker on February 11, 1856, explaining his plans and circumstances. He would lay out a garden of eighteen to twenty acres, three and one half miles from the city center, on undulating land that gently sloped to the southwest. He explained how the weather in Missouri, though extremely cold in winter and hot in the summer, provided good growing conditions for crops such as maize, hemp, and tobacco,

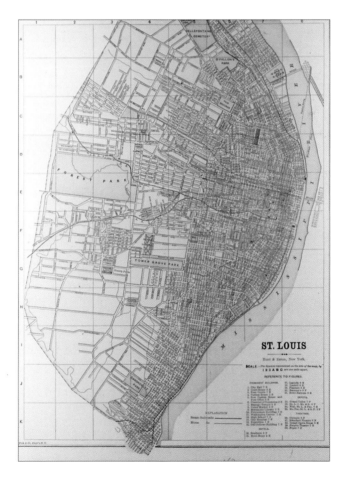

Map of St. Louis and surrounding land, ca. 1870. (Tower Grove Park below center)

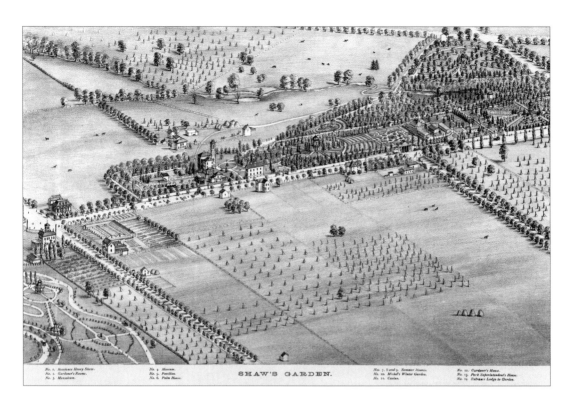

No. 1. *Residence Henry Shaw.*   No. 4. *Museum.*   Nos. 7, 8 and 9. *Summer Houses.*   No. 12. *Gardener's House.*
No. 2. *Gardener's Rooms.*   No. 5. *Pavilion.*   SHAW'S GARDEN.   No. 10. *Mickel's Winter Garden.*   No. 13. *Park Superintendent's House.*
No. 3. *Mausoleum.*   No. 6. *Palm House.*   No. 11. *Casino.*   No. 14. *Entrance Lodge to Garden.*

View of Shaw's Garden. Drawn by Camille Dry, in Pictorial St. Louis, a Topographical Survey Drawn in Perspective *(1875).*

and said that he believed it would make for a successful arbore-tum and fruticetum. He planned to oversee construction of plant houses with southern exposure,[35] and of a curator's house with lecture room and museum, to aid in the promotion of science and taste. They would be separated from the public avenue on the east by an eighty-foot-long wall that would include an entrance gate and small lodge.[36] Despite these certainties, Shaw acknowl-edged that it would be a challenge to find experienced gardeners and a qualified garden superintendent in the Midwest to oversee the garden.

Shaw continued to describe his progress in Missouri in a se-quence of letters to Hooker. In August he wrote of his plan to ring the garden with suburban residences, to be leased as a means of generating income (an idea first used by John Nash at Regent's Park, London, and intended by Paxton at Birkenhead Park, out-side Liverpool).[37] In the following April, 1857, Shaw began actual work on the site, trenching the ground and installing drains, then proceeding with the walls and entrance gate. He wrote Hooker of his interest in putting the land to best use and how he wanted to optimize the view, saying that the arboretum was to be located at a distance from the garden proper and divided into sections of half an acre or more. The arboretum was composed of groups of trees labeled with botanical Latin names—pine trees in the pinetum, oaks in the quercetum, and willows in the salicetum. This composition balanced the fruticetum, which Shaw described as "a vast field of investigation," a "department" of six acres including grapes, plums, and other fruit. He had built a north wall of brick four hundred feet long and a west wall of stone, one thousand feet long and between nine and twelve feet high; the following spring he would add the first plant houses, one hundred fifty

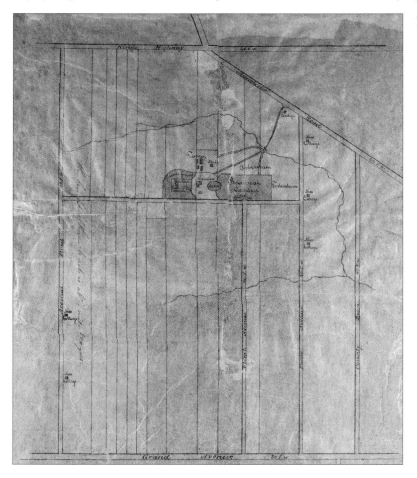

Plan of the land around Tower Grove, ca. 1857.

Garden employees trenching in the fruticetum, ca. 1890.

feet in length, against the north wall.[38] In spite of this progress, Shaw was uncertain about the actual design of the garden's parterres and how to arrange the scientific divisions of the plant world to best promote "a taste for horticultural and rural improvements."[39] In closing he questioned Hooker on the subject.

Hooker's authoritative response was conveyed, in part, by the imprinted seal of the "Royal Gardens Kew" at the top of his stationery. After commending Shaw's progress, Hooker acknowledged the differences between Kew, the "great National Establishment, supported by Government," and the Missouri counterpart, "planned & carried out for the good of the public by a public-spirited *private* gentleman."[40] As a botanist, Hooker considered Shaw's question about the arrangement of plants in garden spaces to be of minor importance. He admitted that there was no single way to plan a garden, and stressed the alliance of practical and aesthetic matters. Consideration of climate and other circumstances, combined with good taste and "convenience of study," were primary concerns—and Victorian priorities—and the details of design were secondary.[41] More importantly a botanical institution needed a good library and museum, which would allow scientists the opportunity to research the subject.[42]

Hooker also suggested a list of the best references, unaware that Shaw already owned them: "Loudon's Cyclopedia of Gardening, McIntosh's Works, Gardener's Magazine and above all the Gardener's Chronicle, a work full of valuable information."[43]

Earlier, in May 1856, Shaw had acted on Hooker's suggestion to use George Engelmann as a botanical adviser. Arrangements were made for Engelmann to travel to Europe for the dual purposes of furthering his own botanical study and collecting books, ideas, and specimens for Shaw (who presumably helped fund the trip). Over the next two years, Engelmann toured the gardens and botanical institutions of Germany, France, Holland, and England. He acquired plans and catalogues and purchased books for the proposed botanical library. Shaw requested several books in particular, including Hooker's Glasgow Royal Botanic Garden catalogue and John Claudius Loudon's "Gardener's Magazines 1st & 2nd series," which he prized for its "valuable information to persons like myself devoted to horticulture and planting."[44] He asked Engelmann to review a particular French treatise on trees, to see if it was similar to Loudon's work on the subject; if so, Humboldt's work should be purchased instead. Engelmann bought seeds for propagation at the garden, as well as dried plants, including the herbarium of European and Asian specimens owned by the German professor Johann Jakob Bernhardi, a collection without equal in the United States and which would become the basis of the garden's holdings. Engelmann was described as having his "eyes wide open," recording information and obtaining a "good notion of what a garden & its contents ought to be."[45] During the trip he visited with colleagues such as Alexander von Humboldt in Berlin, but it was his time with William Hooker, at the Royal Botanic Garden at Kew, that was the highlight of his trip.

"At last at Kew! the great mecca of Botanists and Horticulturalists!" wrote Engelmann.[46] He spent two weeks studying in the "delightfully quiet scientific abode"[47] located outside London on the river Thames near Richmond, on grounds once owned by

The Palm House at Kew. From Chadwick, Works of Sir Joseph Paxton.

Princess Augusta, mother of George III and founder of the botanical garden. He observed plants and toured the Palm House, collecting ideas on architecture and organization. He was given a personal tour of the cactus collection by Hooker, who had given Asa Gray the same tour one year earlier in anticipation of Engelmann's visit. Hooker was delighted to have the expert in North American cacti there to view the institution's holdings, hoping, no doubt, that some of Engelmann's western plants might find their way into the collection.[48] The visit was a success, according to Engelmann: Hooker's "active spirit" he wrote, "is stirring up everything and everybody that comes in contact with him."

While Engelmann traveled in Europe and England, Shaw was busy overseeing progress at the garden. He kept Engelmann informed through letters, explaining how he was anxious to get started and how reading and observation were helping him to gather up "some crumbs of botanical science."[49] He wrote about annuals that had flowered, the condition of trees and shrubs, and how he planned to organize the garden to be symmetrical and elegant.[50] A few months later he wrote of completion of the entrance gate, lodges, and the installation of iron railings. Plant houses were built for the cacti and succulents, which would ulti-

OPPOSITE:
Cactus collection wintered-over in the greenhouse, 1904.

The garden's main gate flanked by Shaw's cactus collection, 1897.

Cacti (Mamillaria) in a changeable bed, to be replaced in spring with tulips and other blooming bulbs, 1905.

mately be placed in impressive changeable beds just inside the main gate, the first sight to greet visitors during warm months. By January 13, 1858, Shaw was no longer focused on the "three grand divisions" of garden, arboretum, and fruticetum, but was busy on the design of individual garden beds. He described one of these parterres, an ornamental garden with radiating paths, complex in nature, that would be used for the systematic arrangement of classified plants. Remaining enthusiastic and busy every day, he confided the need to pace himself so as not to "make a fatigue of a pleasure." At year's end Shaw totaled his expenses for his "great undertaking": $23,000 for the year.

George Engelmann returned from abroad with books, ideas, and plant specimens for use at the garden. But on his return his commitment to the progress of botanical science, fired by Hooker's enthusiasm, underscored the differences between him and Henry Shaw. While at Kew, the two scientists had discussed the needs of Shaw's institution; Asa Gray, too, had agreed that scientific concerns should be foremost in its plans. But Shaw had not been totally swayed by their recommendations. He had, for example, politely rebutted Hooker's suggestion that a library

Garden parterre,
ca. 1890.

and museum must come first, responding that they would have to wait for several years. In spite of their proposals and priorities, he had been planning and planting a garden that put the concerns of the public on the same level of importance as those of science. Shaw had the "ornamental as much at heart as the scientific," Engelmann noted to Gray,[51] and although he praised Shaw's energy and business acumen, in confidence he lamented his lack of scientific education and taste. Shaw's "forsaking" science for aesthetics perplexed Engelmann, who regretted that "scientific botany is secondary or tertiary with him, while I can not get up an enthusiasm for what interests him most."[52] What interested Shaw most was the public and the art of gardening. His vision encompassed all the improvements at Tower Grove—house, garden, and ultimately park—and all the aspects of plan, design, specific plants to be used, and function (not to mention monetary concerns) as they fit into the whole. Engelmann's priorities—an institution committed to science and improving the holdings of the library and herbarium—would be addressed, but not first. The disparity would lessen as Shaw made progress, and Engelmann did concede that the ornamental appealed to the public and would, for better or worse (in his view), "popularize his establishment."[53]

Shaw Finalizes the Plan

Ultimately, Shaw settled on John Claudius Loudon's tripartite method of organization, using his terminology for its classification of parts.[54] In his *Guide to the Garden*, Shaw recorded what is one of the few remaining accounts of the original plan:[55]

> It will be observed the Garden is in three grand divisions.
>
> 1st The Garden proper, containing the plant-houses for tropical and other plants requiring protection, but which in summer are put out of doors, except the ferns and large palms; the Herbaceous ground with plants scientifically arranged and named, is in the centre around the pavillion, and Cacti in the north end of the Garden next the wall.
>
> 2nd The Fruticetum, for shrubbery, and experimental fruit garden.

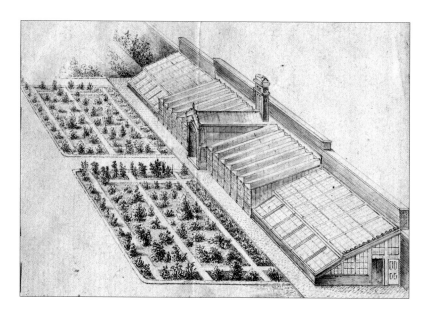

Drawing of the first plant houses on the north wall, ca. 1860.

3rd The Arboretum, containing a collection of Trees comprising all that will
grow in the open air in this climate
and locality; a Pinetum for the pine
family, a Quercetum for oaks, and
Salicetum for willows.[56]

When complete, the botanical garden
consisted of approximately 45 acres, with
the garden proper constituting 9.4 acres, the
fruticetum 8 acres, and the arboretum 20.5,
the balance comprising spaces contiguous to
the villa: the grove (0.6 acres), lawn (2.7),
and vegetable gardens at the rear of the residence (3.5), with pasture land surrounding
the whole.[57] The whole was a right triangle
of land bound by Tower Grove Avenue on
the east, anchored by the Italianate villa on
the south end and the fruticetum to the
north, with the arboretum on a triangular
wedge of acreage to the west. The garden
proper was delineated on the east side by a
stone wall that visually and physically separated it from the woods and farmland beyond. The public garden's first plant house,
along the north wall, employed both ridge-
and-furrow and lean-to roofing to allow a
maximum of sunlight and effectively deflect
midday heat.[58] Close to the villa, to the east,
was the museum building, designed by
George Barnett in 1859, which also housed
the herbarium and library. Just west stood a
rock barn and residence for the manager of
the surrounding farmland.[59] To the south
the private garden that served as Shaw's

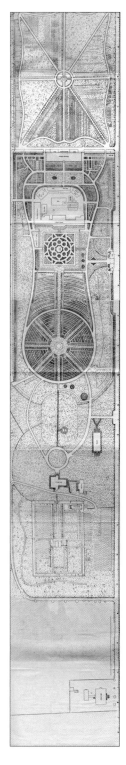

An exact record of Shaw's garden in 1889 with (from north to south) fruticetum, sunken parterre, herbaceous grounds, grove, and vegetable gardens.

Visitors on the steps of the museum building, 1867.

practice grounds remained in place, its range of plant houses and vegetable gardens open to interested visitors into the 1870s.

From the villa tower or balcony, and along the main north-south axis, Shaw could see work below or view the sequence of garden spaces. The line of sight took in the grove, the herbaceous grounds planted in scientific arrangement (the center anchored by an observation pavilion), the drop in elevation to the sunken parterre, and finally the north wall with its plant houses, which marked the southern boundary of the fruticetum. Beyond, a covered seat among the shrubbery echoed the pavilion in the herbaceous grounds. The arboretum to the west, which had pavilions and formal circular plantings that repeated those of the herbaceous grounds, was bounded by Shaw's private drive. The main gate was positioned in the stone wall on the east side of the property, on Tower Grove Avenue, and was aligned with an avenue of silver maples Shaw planted (which would become Flora Boulevard). The shortest (and newest) route from the city led to this public gate.

Shaw's private drive turned back diagonally at the edge of his arboretum on the opposite—northwest—side of the property. It seems Shaw chose to use the established route, possibly the one he had taken into the country as a young man on horseback, out Manchester Road, to get to his estate. Thus he would bypass the public entrance on the east and proceed along the north perimeter of his garden property. This entrance was far removed from the public garden's main gate, and provided views that visitors were not privy to: summer houses, a pond, and the allée of trees he had planted to line his drive. This series of vignettes, images of

View to the grove.

Photo by Carol Betsch.

The Founding of Shaw's Garden **73**

View of the herbaceous grounds.

The pavilion in the fruticetum, ca. 1890.

object and place each artfully arranged by Shaw, welcomed him on his arrival.

As he installed brick and Meramec gravel walks and prepared beds, he also acquired plants. Nearly a decade had passed since he had purchased specimens for his private gardens, and orders for his botanical garden would greatly exceed earlier ones in size and variety. He returned to many of the same sources he had depended on previously and ordered from new ones as well. The nursery of F. K. Phoenix in Bloomington, Illinois, whose promotion of horticulture as patriotic, healthful, educational exercise resonated with Shaw's interests, provided a large assortment of

Sunken parterre in the main garden, looking east toward the main gate, ca. 1860.

The newly planted arboretum, ca. 1866, looking southeast, with Tower Grove House and the main gate in the distance.

The main gate looking north up Tower Grove Avenue, ca. 1890.

*The approach to the garden, then known as Flora Avenue, lined with maples (*Acer dasycarpum)*, ca. 1891.*

Henry Shaw's private gate at the end of Manchester Road, 1908.

The west stone wall of the arboretum, 1905.

A view in the arboretum from Shaw's private drive, with pond and gazebo, 1893.

The stream in the central portion of the arboretum, 1910.

The willow pond in the arboretum, 1892.

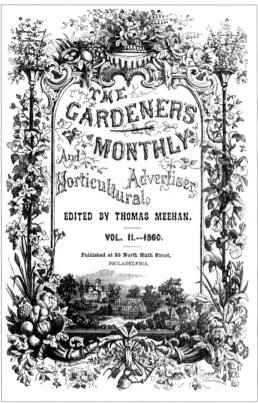

Buist's Almanac and Garden Manual, *1861.*

Meehan's Gardener's Monthly, *1860.*

plants. There were also small orders from East Coast companies, for example B. M. Watson's Old Colony Nursery in Plymouth, Massachusetts, which provided him with weeping cherries, purple beech, and hornbeam. Judging from the size of several 1859–60 orders, he depended most heavily on three sources in the East. Robert Buist, of Philadelphia, supplied seeds of *Ageratum mexicanum*, *Mimosa pudica*, petunia, and issues of Meehan's *Gardener's Monthly* in February 1859; Thomas Meehan, also of Philadelphia, sent an order, and Ellwanger and Barry of Mount Hope Nurseries, Rochester, forwarded a February 1859 order of three hundred hemlock, fifty Norway spruce, and fifty black Austrian pines. Shaw's records indicate amounts, cost, and categories, including "Planta Aqua" (*Nymphaea odorata rubra* and white and purple papyrus), greenhouse plants (*Abutilon* and *Brugmansia*), bedding plants (five sorts of petunias), and specimens (*Barringtonia*, *Wellingtonia gigantea*—the giant redwood or big tree of the Sierra Nevada in California, now called *Sequoiadendron giganteum*—and arum, *Dieffenbachia*).

Shaw ordered and cultivated an astounding number of plants within the first few years of the garden. A single purchase from F. K. Phoenix included over fourteen hundred trees: one hundred white birch, two hundred black walnut, five hundred white elm, two hundred white pine, one hundred tulip trees, one hundred hemlock, and fifty scarlet maples, along with several magnolias, snowball bushes, sweet gum, and Kentucky coffee trees. Thousands of trees and shrubs were planted; "no speedy work," according to Shaw. The number of bulbs, annuals, and cacti used in the changeable beds hints at the labor-intensive gardening popular at the time. Many of the exotic plants were plunged into the ground in pots; all were taken up and replaced each season. Little evidence remains to document precise placement of plants in each section of the garden, but Shaw's records are an exceptional guide to plant preferences and availability in the period. His account book number 36, dated 1859–79, provides a valuable record of the plants used in the Missouri Botanical Garden. The book appears to be a

Cacti in pots in a changeable bed, 1892.

duplication of original orders transcribed into a single volume, a working document that indicates species and variety as ordered from Buist, Ellwanger and Barry, Meehan, Carl Schickler (Stuttgart), Peter Lawson (via Edinburgh), Van der Schoot and Son (Haarlem), Vilmorin Andrieux et Cie (Paris), and Peter Henderson (through his New York City office), and listing plants shared by other institutions such as the Botanic Garden at Washington, D.C., and the Imperial Botanic Garden of St. Petersburg.

Shaw's careful notations in account book 36 also provide information about the habit and cultivation of the plants he chose, such as the need for storage in a "cold house or airy cellar," or to be protected from frost, or planted in dry, sandy soil or in shade. He indicates plants known for their "splendid foliage or showy flowers or gigantic growth," notes their time of flowering, and specifies those that climb, twine, or suit low borders. In one instance he records the three gardeners, Mr. Gurney, E. Locher, and C. Strobel, responsible for specific plantings. Each was furnished with "a list of bulbs under his charge," with labels marked with the appropriate garden number and location. Shaw records the botanical name and order of each plant (perhaps to aid in the "scientific arrangement" of plants, as in the herbaceous grounds), and its survival rate both upon receipt from the company and after planting. Loudon's system of coding with geometrically shaped icons, which appeared in *The Gardener's Magazine* in January 1840, was used to indicate the type and needs of each greenhouse biennial, annual, and perennial, along with their "duration and habitation." These notations (not unlike Thomas Jefferson's garden books) provide insight into Shaw's working method and his hands-on participation in the process.

Shaw used several methods to organize the thousands of plants and trees at the garden. Many of the beds, for example in the herbaceous grounds and in the cactus garden inside the main gate, were arranged by botanical classification and plant type. Shaw also used color theory as an organizational device, planting swaths of like-colored plants and shrubs, as in the red and white

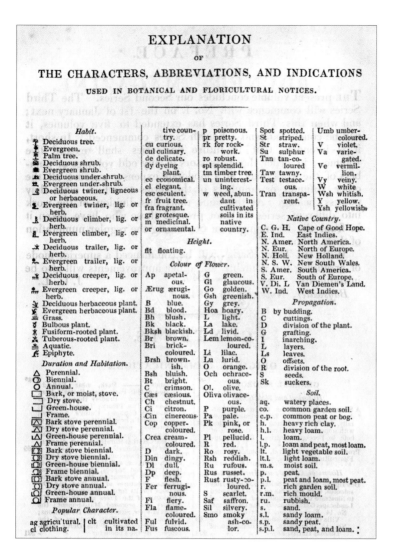

EXPLANATION
OF
THE CHARACTERS, ABBREVIATIONS, AND INDICATIONS
USED IN BOTANICAL AND FLORICULTURAL NOTICES.

Habit.

Deciduous tree.
Evergreen.
Palm tree.
Deciduous shrub.
Evergreen shrub.
Deciduous under-shrub.
Evergreen under-shrub.
Deciduous twiner, ligneous or herbaceous.
Evergreen twiner, lig. or herb.
Deciduous climber, lig. or herb.
Evergreen climber, lig. or herb.
Deciduous trailer, lig. or herb.
Evergreen trailer, lig. or herb.
Deciduous creeper, lig. or herb.
Evergreen creeper, lig. or herb.
Deciduous herbaceous plant.
Evergreen herbaceous plant.
Grass.
Bulbous plant.
Fusiform-rooted plant.
Tuberous-rooted plant.
Aquatic.
Epiphyte.

Duration and Habitation.

△ Perennial.
⊖ Biennial.
○ Annual.
▱ Bark, or moist, stove.
⊔ Dry stove.
⊔ Green-house.
⊔ Frame.
◹ Bark stove perennial.
◸ Dry stove perennial.
◺ Green-house perennial.
◿ Frame perennial.
⊡ Bark stove biennial.
⊡ Dry stove biennial.
⊡ Green-house biennial.
⊡ Frame biennial.
⊡ Bark stove annual.
⊡ Dry stove annual.
⊡ Green-house annual.
⊡ Frame annual.

Popular Character.

ag agricul'tural. | clt cultivated
cl clothing. | in its na-

tive coun-
 try.
cu curious.
cul culinary.
de delicate.
dy dyeing
 plant.
ec economical.
el elegant.
esc esculent.
fr fruit tree.
fra fragrant.
gr grotesque.
m medicinal.
or ornamental.

Height.

flt floating.

Colour of Flower.

Ap apetal-
 ous.
Ærug ærugi-
 nous.
B blue.
Bd blood.
Bh blush.
Bk black.
Bksh blackish.
Br brown.
Bri brick-
 coloured.
Brsh brown-
 ish.
Bsh bluish.
Bt bright.
C crimson.
Cæs cæsious.
Ch chestnut.
Ci citron.
Cin cinereous.
Cop copper-
 coloured.
Crea cream-
 coloured.
D dark.
Din dingy.
Dl dull.
Dp deep.
F flesh.
Fer ferrugi-
 nous.
Fi fiery.
Fla flame-
 coloured.
Ful fulvid.
Fus fuscous.

p poisonous.
pr pretty.
rk for rock-
 work.
ro robust.
spl splendid.
tm timber tree.
un uninterest-
 ing.
w weed, abun-
 dant in
 cultivated
 soils in its
 native
 country.

G green.
Gl glaucous.
Go golden.
Gsh greenish.
Gy grey.
Hoa hoary.
L light.
La lake.
Ld livid.
Lem lemon-co-
 loured.
Li lilac.
Lu lurid.
O orange.
Och ochrace-
 ous.
Ol. olive.
Oliva olivace-
 ous.
P purple.
Pa pale.
Pk pink, or
 rose.
Pl pellucid.
R red.
Ro rosy.
Rsh reddish.
Ru rufous.
Rus russet.
Rust rusty-
 loured.
S scarlet.
Saf saffron.
Sil silvery.
Smo smoky
 ash-co-
 lor.

Spot spotted.
St striped.
Str straw.
Su sulphur
Tan tan-co-
 loured
Taw tawny.
Test testace-
 ous.
Tran transpa-
 rent.

Umb umber-
 coloured.
V violet.
Va varie-
 gated.
Ve vermil-
 lion.
Vy veiny.
W white
Wsh whitish.
Y yellow.
Ysh yellowish.

Native Country.

C. G. H. Cape of Good Hope.
E. Ind. East Indies.
N. Amer. North America.
N. Eur. North of Europe.
N. Holl. New Holland.
N. S. W. New South Wales.
S. Amer. South America.
S. Eur. South of Europe.
V. Di. L. Van Diemen's Land.
W. Ind. West Indies.

Propagation.

B by budding.
C cuttings.
D division of the plant.
G grafting.
I inarching.
L layers.
Ls leaves.
O offsets.
R division of the root.
S seeds.
Sk suckers.

Soil.

aq. watery places.
co. common garden soil.
c.p. common peat or bog.
h. heavy rich clay.
h.l. heavy loam.
l. loam.
l.p. loam and peat, most loam.
lt. light vegetable soil.
lt.l. light loam.
m.s. moist soil.
p. peat.
p.l. peat and loam, most peat.
r. rich garden soil.
r.m. rich mould.
ru. rubbish.
s. sand.
s.l. sandy loam.
s.p. sandy peat.
s.p.l. sand, peat, and loam.

Loudon's system of coding plant type and habit as illustrated in The Gardener's Magazine, *January 1840, and used by Shaw.*

border of his private garden. He recorded flowers by the color of their bloom for use as a planting guide; one list cites plants with red, yellow, cerise, and purple blossoms. Illustrations and early photographs reveal visual pattern as another basis of organization. The circular configuration of the herbaceous grounds was reinforced with row after row of plant material, divided by paths radiating from the center which created eight wedge-shaped sections. The square sunken parterre contained circular and triangular beds that, when perceived as a unit, mimicked the shape of a snowflake or star. The fruticetum's rectangular shape was soft-

Garden beds organized by plant type: a mix of cacti at the main gate, 1898.

Flower bed planting organized in paisley motif, 1891.

ened at the edges by circuit walks that flowed around the perimeter, but the cross axes were reinforced by arrow-straight paths
from corner to corner. Even trees in the arboretum were planted
in rows, strengthening its affinity to a nursery (which was one of
its uses) rather than to natural woods.[60] This linear planting created a strong visual pattern, one that evokes the custom of planting trees in quincunx formations, a practice Shaw would have
known from his European travels and his appreciation of Renaissance art.[61] Such arrangement was decorative in effect but also facilitated study, underscoring resemblances and differences
between plants.[62] By organizing groups of like plants into rows,
with paths to each side of the beds, one could view specimens with
greatest clarity. The use of uniform rows as an ordering device allowed visitors to view plants from both sides and as the garden

*Ribbon bedding
planted with
alternating rows of
Echeveria, 1910.*

The strong visual patterns and decorative effect of the sunken parterre and herbaceous grounds, ca. 1870.

could be viewed not only up close but from above, from the observatory pavilion, the visual patterning could be seen to best effect.[63]

Garden structures contributed to the overall decorative effect. Made of similar materials and using similar motifs, many were variations on a theme, and the themes were fanciful and exotic in flavor rather than classical. The two-story observation pavilion in the center of the herbaceous grounds and the covered seat in the fruticetum shared scalloped, finlike ripples on their bulbous, domed roofs. Lacy carpenter's gothic fretwork dripped from the roof's edges. Brick was used in the primary (herbaceous grounds) pavilion, and secondary seats were made of lattice.[64] Arbors shared the same elements and construction: walls of lattice, and lateral beams that functioned as a pergola, with lacy wooden trim.[65] These fanciful structures were draped with climbers or shrouded by shrubs, enhancing their evocative effect. A reciprocity among four "sister" pavilions served as a visual repeat that strengthened the design and reinforced for the viewer—via decorative effects—parts within the whole.

For his sunken parterre Shaw copied the plan for a "select flower-garden" as illustrated in Loudon's *Encyclopedia*, illustration number 862. According to the author, the square bed, con-

TOP LEFT: Pavilion at western edge of the garden.

TOP RIGHT: One of two covered seats, or "pagodas," in the fruticetum.

Observatory pavilion overlooking the herbaceous grounds and sunken parterre.
All from Inland Monthly, *1872.*

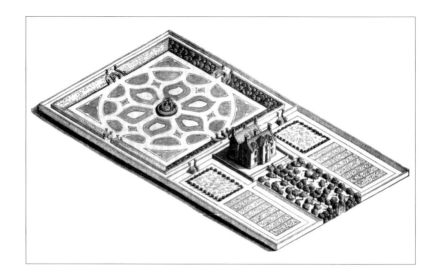

sisting of circles and pointed compartments, lends itself for use as a "select," "American," or "changeable" garden depending on the plants used. Loudon identified it as a garden in Heidelberg, Germany (without any other specific information), and Shaw may have seen the original on his visits there in 1845 and 1851.[66] The garden illustrated in the encyclopedia was planted with orange trees; photographs suggest that the Missouri version was planted via the technique of bedding out, probably using annuals grown in Shaw's greenhouses, the plants similar in height and shape but varying in color. The general organization of Shaw's parterre is also strikingly similar to illustration number 200 in Loudon's 1838 *Suburban Gardener*, addressed in the section on designs for small country villas.[67] Loudon suggests the placement of fruit trees or small vegetable gardens around the villa and a "sunk flower-garden, consisting of a variety of curvilinear beds, bordered by a kerb of stone, and surrounded by turf" with paired staircases that descend from the terrace (as at Shaw's garden).

Not everything was finished when the garden officially opened on June 15, 1859; beds were still in the process of being filled, and work was being "pushed forward as rapidly as is consistent with true arrangement."[68] Engelmann, waiting for the completion of the library and museum Shaw had promised, judged that the place could "not be called a garden yet."[69] Still, an assortment of visitors came, first signing the guest book Shaw had provided: a state senator and his family, groups of women, out-of-town guests from nearby Ste. Genevieve and as far away as Rochester, New York. Inside the entrance were urns filled with exotic specimens, trees shipped from California, Africa, and Asia, and decorative arched openings that led to the fruticetum. Shaw's Black Hamburg grapes, which he had planted six years before, hung from large, full branches, espaliered fig trees were trained against the stone wall; and pineapples and lemons were ripening in the plant houses.

The one major distraction that Shaw had had to confront in 1858–59 had been a breach of promise lawsuit brought against him by Effie Carstang, who claimed he had broken his promise of marriage to her.[70] His excitement about the garden's completion was tempered by this very public litigation that would not

Gardeners preparing fig plants along the west wall for winter, October 30, 1891.

end for another year, but still he found a way to celebrate its opening by commissioning the artist Emil Herziger to paint his portrait. Using the traditional method of conflating the image of the subject with his life's work, it illustrates Shaw in his role as garden patron and planner, in a symbolic gathering together of the new garden buildings and his favorite plants. Within the composition the entrance gate, the museum building, and the north wall plant houses (the portrait is one of only two remaining illustrations of them) surround Shaw, who stands with architectural or planting plans rolled in one hand. Plants representative

Watercolor portrait of Henry Shaw in 1859, the year the garden opened to the public, by Emil Herziger.

of his interests and the garden's collection fill the scene—a cactus, referring to George Engelmann; a rose, Shaw's favorite flower; and a pine tree, a reference to his arboretum or possibly to the pinyon pine he had sent to Kew in 1857.

Professional Staff and Monumental Improvements

A major round of improvements was under way at the garden within a decade, including the construction of the grand glass-and-iron plant house Shaw had planned and the completion of the second story of the museum building.[71] The need for improved propagation and exhibition space, the desire to make a more monumental statement, and the practical necessity of having a team of professionals to oversee the hands-on work of gardening prompted Shaw to add buildings and staff. This last concern was possibly most pressing, as a project of the scope of this garden demanded the labor of an experienced workforce. As early as 1857 Shaw had acknowledged his inability to oversee everything himself. In England and Europe he had seen the manpower needed for planting and maintenance on a large scale. He understood that a good gardener must be a person of experience and observations and could not be educated in a year or two.[72] Finding qualified horticultural help was the most difficult problem for Shaw, in part because of his location, but more so because it was a general American problem. His comment that "the profession is sadly undervalued" in the United States was a just assessment of the state of the profession at midcentury.[73]

Luckily, in 1867, an Englishman named James Gurney approached him about a position. Gurney came equipped not only with a knowledge of botany and horticulture but with the ability to oversee a large number of gardeners and manage an undertaking the size of Shaw's garden. From Newport, Buckinghamshire, Gurney (1831–1920) had come to the United States

James Gurney in the arboretum.

in 1866, bringing with him experience acquired over four years at the Royal Botanic Society's garden at Regent's Park, London, working under garden curator Robert Marnock. According to Gurney, his earliest work was with the merchant florist James Atkins at his home, Prairie College, Northampton, and at the Handsworth nurseries, near Shaw's hometown of Sheffield.[74] His particular interest in nymphaean botany, or water lilies, may have come from his experience working with the plant collection at Woburn, Bedfordshire, for the seventh duke of Bedford.[75] Gurney apparently took little time to prove himself to Shaw. He first appears in the time book in August 1867 at the wage of $22 per month, his rate increasing to $40 within three months. Shaw and Gurney worked side by side from 1867, Shaw directing, Gurney planting and serving as superintendent of the garden.[76] Besides their passion for horticulture, Gurney and Shaw shared similarly retiring dispositions, and both were soft-spoken.[77]

Shaw not only respected Gurney's ability, he considered him a friend.

Gurney's contribution is important to the history of Tower Grove, and his descendants assumed management positions, continuing the Gurney name into the twentieth century.[78] During his long tenure at the garden, the family moved about the property, living in a two-story house at the arboretum gate, near what later became the junction of Vandeventer and Shaw Avenue, and then just south of the garden, on the edge of Tower Grove Park in what is still in use today as the park director's house, at the corner of Tower Grove and Magnolia Avenues. Gurney could always be found in the palm house documenting agaves, araucarias, ficus, and ferns, or around the lily ponds. His hand is evident in the documentation of plant lists, a job he shared with Shaw, particularly as the owner aged. He led a fair-sized crew of gardeners, one that increased to forty in the summer months, as

James Gurney (upper left) with his crew of gardeners at Tower Grove, July 12, 1890.

attested to by time sheets and photographs.[79] Early accounts refer to these workers as Bohemian immigrants; some of them were fathers and sons from the large German population of St. Louis at the time. Photographs capture Gurney at ease on nasturtium-patterned garden seats, possibly those Shaw ordered from Coalbrookdale, England; fashionably positioned atop giant water lilies; and proudly at attention among his team of employees.

Gurney's botanical contribution was in the area of water lily propagation and cultivation. Joseph Paxton had successfully coaxed the giant *Victoria* into bloom at Chatsworth in 1849 (and was knighted for being the first to do so), marking the real beginning of water lily mania in England; countless amateur gardeners and experts, as well as Queen Victoria herself, were infatuated with their exoticism.[80] The plant's enormous leaves, which can grow to six feet in diameter and hold afloat many pounds of weight, are supported by an inflated network of ribs below the water surface. Their blooms, which change in color from white to pink to red, last only forty-eight hours. As their increased use in botanical and public gardens spread to the United States and ultimately to the Midwest, Gurney's expertise in the area of breeding became celebrated. His success in creating a tricolor striped lily (red, white, and blue) established him as an important contributor to the field. (Many new tropical water lilies were bred in the 1920s and 1930s at the Missouri Botanical Garden, where they are still featured today.)

Architectural additions and the "proper accessories" Shaw spoke of were an important part of the improvements made between 1867 and 1889. Most important was the construction of the 1868 glass palm house based, according to Shaw, on Paxton's Chatsworth conservatory and the Crystal Palace in London, which was erected just south of the original row of plant houses along the north wall. Of a scale and design befitting an important institution, this main conservatory stood adjacent to the sunken parterre and provided a visual terminus for the garden's primary axis. It provided dramatic improvement over the first plant

Garden visitors enjoying the Victoria regia *pool.*

The fashionable practice of having one's picture taken on a Victoria *lily pad, 1890.*

houses, which primarily addressed function over aesthetics, and it furnished increased exhibition space in terms of both height and breadth. Its three-part configuration consisted of a predominant central bay, with ridge-and-furrow roof extensions and secondary sloped glasshouses attached at each side. A glass hip roof, strikingly similar to that at the Sheffield Botanical Garden, topped a range of arched windows that ran the length of the facade. "Glory to God in the Highest and on Earth Peace, Good Will Toward Men" was inscribed along the front.

The size of this grand new conservatory was increased by incorporating the first plant houses at the garden.[81] The flexibility and convenience of iron and glass buildings, which could be taken down and reassembled, had been demonstrated on a large scale when the Crystal Palace was disassembled and moved to Sydenham after the closing of the Great Exhibition in Hyde Park in 1851. Such reuse was not only practical and economical, it was a modern approach to building, contrasting with the permanence of traditional architecture that took long periods of time to build and remained on a given site. This innovative approach, a kind of recycling of building parts, made perfect sense to Shaw. By removing those "that stood against the wall and putting them in range with the palm house," Shaw reused the earliest glasshouses from the original north wall location at the new conservatory site. The move helped create a space where succulents, ferns, and cacti could be exhibited under one roof, which soon became the very heart of the garden.

Nearby, a secondary brick conservatory, known today as the Linnean House, was designed by George Barnett and erected in 1882. Built on the recently cleared site of the first plant houses along the north wall, it made reference to English models Shaw knew, both Nicholas Hawksmoor's 1705 orangery at Kensington Palace and John Nash's 1830 conservatory (one of four moved from Buckingham Palace to Kew in 1836). In its primary use of brick and minimal use of glass, the Linnean House clearly looked to the past rather than the future. As with its predeces-

sors, its main function was to allow wintering over of plants (housing those not hardy to Missouri, including camellias, as it still does today), and it also served as a site for public events and exhibitions. Ornamented with crisp brickwork surrounding the fan-lighted entry, a facade motif of alternating arched windows and pilasters, and topped with busts of the botanists Linnaeus, Thomas Nuttall, and Asa Gray, the structure has been in continuous use since 1882. The 1868 conservatory and the Linnean House reinforced the north end of the garden; perpendicular to the main axis, they served as a visual (and in a sense physical) "stop," contributing, over time, to reduced use of the fruticetum just to the north.

Some of the finest early photographs of the garden, from 1868 through the turn of the century, were taken near the main conservatory and the Linnean House. One senses the importance of this place in the hierarchy of spaces at the garden—it was a favorite spot for recording one's visit. Here countless people posed to have their likeness recorded: young women with arms akimbo,

The Linnean House and pool with Victoria regia *water lilies.*

The 1868 main conservatory (with plant houses moved from their original north wall location), looking north, 1890.

View of the parterre with Juno, looking south from the main conservatory, 1890.

couples frozen in midstep, children overtaken by giant fronds. Framed by the hedged herbaceous grounds, visitors stood in a kaleidoscopic array of gardenesque plantings, ribbon borders accentuated by exotic palms and yuccas, thousands of dazzling massed annuals, and (later) ponds afloat with the colossal veined leaves and nodding buds of nymphaea. A benevolent marble Juno, commissioned by Shaw in 1886 and sculpted by the Italian Carlo Nicoli, stood as a beacon mooring the central bed of the sunken parterre.[82] Her gaze was fixed south toward Shaw's villa, and at her feet her name was spelled out in a script of contrasting annuals. Besides representing Shaw's taste, these early gardens and their aesthetic represent the culmination of a century of experimentation with new plant types and methods of planting that best displayed their unique characteristics. The profusion of color and pattern, bounded by stone walls and surrounded by countryside, juxtaposed nature and culture in a contrast as clear as that between orchids and haystacks.

Because a primary goal of the garden was to educate the public, Shaw wrote a guide that outlined its history and use. More than a list of directives or rules, the *Guide to the Missouri Botanical Garden* instructed the public on this garden's arrangement and history, and on the role of the garden in society.[83] It began with a description of the landscape when Shaw first visited in 1820, comparing the site's original state with the artistic and scientific creation it had become, and outlining the evolution of the garden from inception to completion. In it Shaw recommended the three "grand divisions" needed to make a successful botanical garden—the garden proper or "systematic arrangement of classified plants," a fruticetum, and an arboretum. Included within the whole would be an American garden (plants native to this continent), a palm house and plant houses for exotics, a botanical museum, and a reference library.

The guide educated visitors on various kinds of gardens, including "florist" gardens[84] and nurseries, as a contrast to the subject of botany as a science. At the same time, it suggested the contemporary overlap of two fields of interest—horticulture and botany—which explains the use of certain terms, such as "garden botany." Shaw addressed landscape gardening as an art that teaches how to lay out grounds, plant woods, and dispose water to the best advantage. The guide included six regulations, similar to the rules at the Kew gardens, which banned picnicking, alcohol, and animals; these helped protect the grounds, and were necessary since thousands of visitors benefited from free admission.

Shaw believed that botanical gardens were among the most important institutions of a civilized country. Their contribution to science and their economic application aside, he recognized their ability to cultivate taste in the mainstream of the population. The improvement of nature was synonymous with the improvement of society, and a botanical garden should

> stimulate all amateurs in the city and State to plant ornamental trees and shrubs not generally found in their immediate vicinities; so that all our gardens and pleasure grounds, might take their tone from this central emporium, and induce the planting of those magnificent and enduring ornaments of nature. A botanical collection open to the public, acts as a stimulus to ornament and beautify our country; for to see fine plants and trees is far more persuasive and satisfactory, than a picture or description of them however elaborate.

One objective of his garden, then, was to serve as a model for an improved society, to prompt citizens to participate actively in the "botanical improvement" of the environment, which, in turn, would spur progress and serve as the beginning step in the advancement of the country and its entire population.

Beyond the goals of education and improvement, the garden was meant to entertain. It succeeded in this; visitors and the press

Visitors on the grass walk linking the main conservatory and the observatory in the herbaceous grounds, 1890.

Crowds of visitors enjoying the garden, 1890. Photo by E. Boehl.

The Founding of Shaw's Garden   **99**

praised the garden, often in rapturous narrative. Travelers' guides and atlases embraced this place of floral beauty, considered the new center of the world of garden botany, for its plethora of exotic plants, from heliotrope to India rubber trees, and for its mission of serving the public good. Written accounts, often with zealous overtones, continued for decades after the official opening. The garden was included in publications such as *The Stranger's Guide to St. Louis* (1867) and *Compton's Pictorial St. Louis* (1875). Dacust and Buel's *Tour of St. Louis* (1878) likened Shaw's garden to the monuments of Europe, citing it as that "one object of supreme interest" that exists in cities of importance.[85] *The City of Saint Louis of Today* (1889) described the garden beds as the choicest of nature's selections, emulating "sapphires—in clusters of brilliants and flowers."[86]

Shaw's project was a subject of interest in accounts at the national and international level as well. A compilation of garden features was illustrated in *Frank Leslie's Illustrated News* and *The Illustrated Journal of Agriculture* (ca. 1879–82), and Charles Mason Hovey's Boston-based *Magazine of Horticulture* included an article on it as early as 1859. Thomas Meehan, the Philadelphia publisher of *The Gardener's Monthly and Horticultural Advertiser*, described each portion of the garden in August 1868, judging the whole to be "unequalled by anything of the kind in the United States," and praised Shaw's aim to educate through botany and horticulture, planting those "first germs of usefullness" in the mind of the public. Meehan noted that Shaw's greatest pleasure was in observing this educational process and in his knowledge of "the immense power such refined influences have on the general happiness of mankind."[87] Not only public education but botany as a field of professional study benefited from the garden's steady growth as an institution. The British publication *The Gardener's Chronicle* acknowledged the potential of the St. Louis facility as the "the botanical centre of the New World."[88] William Cullen Bryant's epic recording of America's natural and cultural landmarks, *Picturesque America* (1874), included Shaw's garden in the text and as part of an illustrated vignette of the city's cultural institutions, confirming its status as a local treasure of national importance. With his typical fervor, Bryant applauded the extensive botanical garden, conservatory, and collection made up of "every variety of tree, shrub, and plant, that can be grown in this country by natural or artificial means," praising, too, its contribution to St. Louis, a city "destined for a great future."[89]

In the early years of the garden, visitors came from near and far.[90] To those in charge of keeping the paths tidy and the grounds well groomed, the number of visitors must have seemed staggering. Shaw could not have been more pleased. He wrote to Asa Gray that forty thousand visitors in forty days had entered the main gate. Attendance figures were often recorded in the thousands (numbers reaching thirty thousand for special events have been quoted). The garden was open daily except for Sunday (some critics felt this closure was at odds with Shaw's vision of serving the public). Two special openings per year, the first Sundays in June and September, drew huge numbers—for example, one Sunday in September 1891, when sixteen thousand visitors were recorded. Special events such as chrysanthemum exhibitions, set up under tents, prompted return visits and long lines.

Family, friends, and colleagues of Henry Shaw, important politicians, writers, and, of course, botanists toured the grounds. Many signed Shaw's gold-tooled leather autograph album after sharing tea or claret with the owner. The list of distinguished visitors is as varied and colorful as a bed of exotic flowers. The editor Horace Greeley, Mrs. George Armstrong Custer, P. T. Barnum, and the writer Charles Kingsley all came, as did the coauthors of *The Gilded Age*, Samuel Clemens (better known as Mark Twain) and Charles Dudley Warner. The horticulturist Robert Buist traveled from Philadelphia in September 1876 to check on the plants his nursery had supplied. Joseph Dalton Hooker and Louis Agassiz both visited. Hooker, on his way west to survey flora in Colorado and accompanied by his traveling partner Asa Gray, stopped to assess the results of his father's guidance two decades earlier.

Garden staff transporting plants for donation to charities after one of the many chrysanthemum shows held on the garden grounds, 1907.

One visitor was in a particularly good position to critique the garden. Traveling through the Midwest in the spring of 1863 as secretary of the United States Sanitary Commission, and after initial work on New York's Central Park, Frederick Law Olmsted toured the grounds. He noted that his visit to St. Louis was of great interest and value, but his assessment of Shaw's garden, as recorded in a letter dated April 4, was frankly uncomplimentary: a disappointment, he described it, a "dwarfish and paltry affair."[91] His criticism was indicative of radical changes in taste that were to manifest themselves in designed spaces across the country, including Tower Grove, after Shaw's death. But while Olmsted was still in the city Shaw took him to a stretch of land just south of the garden to discuss the project he was about to begin, a public park that would serve as an aesthetic and recreational complement to the garden. Olmsted commended the site's "majestic simplicity of surface," and acknowledged that it would make for a "park of noble breadth and delicious repose of character."

3

"To Unite Utility, Variety and Beauty"

TOWER GROVE PARK

In all ornamental improvements of land the purposes for which these improvements are intended are the first objects of the Landscape Gardener.

—HENRY SHAW, *Plan of the Park and Reasons for Its Adoption* (ca. 1870)

The effects of the Civil War were felt in St. Louis soon after Shaw's garden opened to the public. Property values fell 75 percent, idle steamboats lined the levee, and order was enforced by martial law. George Engelmann speculated that the garden, located on an elevated plain with its substantial buildings and protective stone wall, might become a battleground—a "great prize to be fought for."[1] Even if the war made for "slow going" at the garden, Shaw remained busy at work with landscape improvements and plants. He spent cold days in February 1862 recording the various sizes and blooms of a long list of exotics flourishing "under glass" in one of the plant houses. In the winter of 1863–64, however, a record freeze of 22 degrees below zero claimed a large percentage of the plants Shaw had nurtured; in his journal, he accounted for each grape, pine, cedar, vine, and fruit that had been lost. Replacements were ordered, and in April 1867 Asa Gray sent seeds from Kew and Australia. Shaw spent time composing two large scrapbooks—personal herbaria—for Misses Mary Brooks and Mary Harris, young daughters of neighbors in the city. A beautiful means of educating the young women about botany, the scrapbooks contained pressed flowers from around the world—variegated calceolaria (the wildly popular "pocket-book plant"), trillium, abutilon, peony, and rose-colored seaweed "from the Potomac" framed with gold and white paper lace, each labeled with its proper name.

In the spring of 1868, as the first major improvements were being completed at the garden, Shaw shifted his focus to the public park he had contemplated for seventeen years. But before he could begin shaping the park there were political and practical obstacles to deal with. As the benefactor, Shaw hoped to persuade the city to become partners in the venture. To avoid possible conflict created by municipal politics he laid out a clear means of financing, governing, and maintaining the new public institution—a method of oversight and management that remains in place today. He thus made a proposition to Mayor James S. Thomas: he would donate the land to the city, and in return the city would provide funds, based on Shaw's recommendations, for its improvement and maintenance into the future. That the land lay 660 feet outside the city limits at the time was a minor formality; St. Louis had grown to the edge of Shaw's property and clearly would soon extend beyond the proposed site. The existing charter limited the city's authority on such decisions, however, so the proposal was brought before the Missouri legislature. After approval of city and state officials the property was annexed into the city, and on March 9, 1867, an act was passed authorizing the park and establishing a board of commissioners, to be appointed by the state supreme court.[2] The following October Shaw gave his "princely gift" of 276.76 acres

to the city of St. Louis.[3] A special bond issue earmarked $360,000 for the park's initial development, and the city agreed to allot $25,000 annually for maintenance and improvement. With legal and financial matters in place, Shaw could think about aesthetics and planning, bringing together his experience with the botanical garden, his appreciation for parks as vehicles of social reform, and his increased knowledge about park planning in England and America.

Shaw, and America, Look to British Models

In 1844 Charles Mason Hovey, editor of the Boston publication the *Magazine of Horticulture*, visited the new Derby Arboretum in England. On his return he wrote of the need for such public spaces in this country—"public gardens *free to all* in crowded towns and cities."[4] Seven years later Frederick Law Olmsted similarly noted that democratic America had no equivalent to the "People's Garden," Birkenhead Park, near Liverpool, which he had just visited. A. J. Downing, too, wrote about the need for parks as a reprieve from city life. Increasingly, newspapers and journals discussed green space for the enjoyment of all people and acknowledged the creation of parks as the "next great step" in the refinement of America.[5]

Reformers and advocates such as the writer William Cullen Bryant, who praised London city parks for their contribution to health and happiness, rallied for the creation of public spaces. Advocates believed that parks served purposes greater than recreation and respite. They educated people's taste and sensibility and promoted equality by creating places where the millionaire and the mill worker could walk the same grounds. Like libraries and museums, parks fulfilled a social duty by contributing to society's improvement. Their particular importance to America was, as Olmsted's collaborator Calvert Vaux put it, their ability to translate "democratic ideas into trees and dirt." As cities and local governments began earmarking funds and identifying urban lots and wasteland for improvement, the debate focused on the requirements of a public park—defining proper location, rules of behavior, and visual effect.

These issues had begun to be addressed in Britain's newly formed parks. Developed as a response to the negative impact of the Industrial Revolution and urban growth, new green space eased the problems created by increased population and industry. Referred to as the "lungs of the city," parks provided breathing room for the occupants of Britain's dirty and densely crowded metropolitan areas. As places for passive and active recreation they provided an alternative to unhealthy diversions, and as educational spaces they provided both moral and practical instruction and addressed the concern for improvement on a personal and societal level. Perhaps most important, these nineteenth-century parks were created for the working class, a distinction that separated them from pleasure grounds of the past. Neither private nor royal grounds adapted for public use (such as Hyde Park in London), they were created specifically for a middle-class public that, for the first time in history, need not have money or connections in order to use them. That the factory worker or baker and his family would have equal access to and sense of ownership in these new spaces was the defining characteristic.

Americans did not yet have public parks, but they were using another type of outdoor space for recreation and restoration. "Garden cemeteries," whose main purpose was to provide a hygienic and pleasant atmosphere for burial, also provided pleasurable surroundings for those who visited. As the earliest public spaces to be shaped in accordance with principles of landscape design, these cemeteries were appreciated as places to commune, not only with those who had passed on, but with friends and family, and with nature. This recreational aspect is seen in the prototype, Mount Auburn in Cambridge, Massachusetts (est. 1831), which combined eclectic monuments, plantings, vistas, and even an experimental garden, within its 173 wooded acres. Picturesque garden cemeteries, sometimes referred to as "rural cemeteries" for

their location outside cities, were developed in Brooklyn (Green-Wood, 1838), Cincinnati (Spring Grove, 1845) and St. Louis, where Bellefontaine Cemetery, begun in 1849, spread over a rolling, wooded bluff that overlooked the Mississippi River.[6] With their romantic associations, sculptural monuments, and curving pathways, these were the predecessors of public parks in America.

In 1849 Downing wrote about the relationship between cemeteries and parks as places of natural beauty, as outdoor drawing rooms for social interaction. His ideas reflect the seminal writings of John Claudius Loudon, whose 1843 publication *On Laying Out, Planting, and Managing of Cemeteries* shaped practice on both sides of the Atlantic.[7] Loudon addressed the practical and health issues regarding burial grounds and suggested that large areas of ground near cities should be preserved for dual purposes—as breathing places to be used as parks or cemeteries as dictated by need. He argued that cemeteries should be not only soothing and dignified but educational spaces that would improve a person's "moral sentiments" and the level of taste in the general public. Pointing to the example of Abney Park Cemetery, London, its arboretum supplied by the preeminent Loddiges family nursery (and laid out alphabetically), he suggested that these places be planted like arboreta or botanical gardens and that specimens should be labeled for the enlightenment of those who visited. Certain trees were chosen for their symbolism: weeping varieties of willow and cypress (used in burial sites since antiquity) as well as pines and cedars (evergreens that do not appear to die each winter). According to Loudon, the need for grounds to be practical and utilitarian dictated a particular method of planting known as the gardenesque, and discouraged the imitation of wild nature that was referred to as the picturesque. Consequently, he promoted the use of single specimen trees set within the landscape for the clean, hygienic impression they conveyed, and rejected thickets of shrubbery and irregular plantings, which seemed disorderly by comparison. The relationship between the design of cemeteries and that of parks is apparent in Loudon's illustrations of grounds planted in the "cemetery style" or the "pleasure ground style."

British practitioners were responsible for developing various different kinds of landscape spaces at midcentury. Robert Marnock's projects in Sheffield included Weston Park, the Sheffield Botanic Garden, and the General Cemetery (1836).

Illustration of the "Cemetery Style" from Loudon's On the Laying Out, Planting, and Meaning of Cemeteries . . . *(1843), sent to Shaw by the author.*

Joseph Paxton planned Coventry Cemetery in 1847, the year his Birkenhead Park opened, and was responsible for the collection of trees and shrubs at the influential Chatsworth arboretum. Such mass plantings were becoming a popular alternative to the conservatory as a means of enjoying nature and learning about botany. Education and experience, Paxton believed, would increase the public's interest in tree and shrub collections over ornamental elements such as sculpture and flower beds, and ultimately cultivate interest in parklike spaces.

Joseph Paxton made many changes at Chatsworth to please the sixth duke of Devonshire and his visiting public. The estate was updated with additions such as the Rockeries, a unique variation on the standard rock garden which blended art and geology, composed of rocks dragged to the site and assembled into colossal forms that ornamented the forest. He refurbished the Willow Tree fountain (the "Squirting Tree," as the thirteen-year-old future queen Victoria called it)[8] and added the 264-foot Emperor Fountain, which paid tribute to Victorian invention (and remains the highest gravity-flow fountain in the world). But the most fashionable contributions in this nineteenth-century updating of Chatsworth were the eight-acre pinetum, in 1829, and the arboretum, in 1835, its forty acres of 1,670 species arranged by family and including walks, ponds, and a grotto.

An article on the Chatsworth arboretum, along with the plan and plant list, was published in the August 1835 issue of *The Gardener's Magazine*, accompanied by the comments of editor John Claudius Loudon.[9] The article outlines the procedure for planting an arboretum for small places of two to three acres and for country residences of a hundred acres and more. Plantings were to be organized by "grand divisions" or, as Loudon described them, the "links which form the chain of orders" recognized by botanists and published in the *Hortus Britannicus*. At Chatsworth the arboretum was to be viewed along the length of a mile-long walk; the pinetum was near the grotto because of the warm microclimate there; and a third grouping, the salicetum (the botanical Latin term for a willow collection), was located near a pond to utilize the damp ground. The article also discusses the role of arboreta in society, including their social importance as symbols of progress, and their elevation of landscape gardening to a higher degree of artistic refinement. By placing in the public mind the "first germs of a taste for trees and shrubs," the arboretum was also important in its ability to cultivate taste.

It was in the late 1830s, soon after the development of the arboretum at Chatsworth, that serious discussion began about urban conditions and the pressing need for public parks. Birkenhead Park, across the river Mersey from Liverpool, planned by Paxton and laid out by the landscape gardener Edward Kemp, was to become a model for later parks in both England and America. One of the first large parks (125 acres) planned to benefit all classes of people, it provided the public the opportunity for fresh air and recreation amid beautiful natural surroundings just three miles from the city center. An 1843 Improvement Act authorized the purchase of land to be repaid by taxpayers, and the laying out and planting was complete by 1847; the park opened on Easter Monday of that year. The mounded topography, lakes, and indigenous trees were supplemented by decorative plantings of *Pinus radiata* (Monterey pine) from California, evocative weeping willows, and poplars. Paxton added an exotic assortment of bridges and architecture, ranging from Swiss and Italianate to Roman and Gothic. Such an eclectic mix of buildings and style was to be repeated in countless nineteenth-century parks.

That Shaw looked to Birkenhead for ideas is evident in similarities, both ideological and concrete, between it and Tower Grove Park. First, both were within arm's reach of, yet outside, a dense urban center. Before the creation of the park, the Birkenhead land was swampy, and its views were of an industrial cityscape. Paxton's solution to these problems was to drain and build up the ground, creating mounds and plantings that screened the view and provided a sense of enclosure and separation from the broader setting while also making the land suitable for planting. Although Shaw did not yet have to deal with an urban, industrial perimeter, he knew, based on its growth over previous decades, that the city would soon surround the park. The condition of the Tower Grove site was not as problematic—it was a stretch of prairie without large springs or ponds and with only a few mature trees.

Second, the innovative plan for circulation systems used at Birkenhead was applied at Tower Grove (as it was at Central Park and elsewhere in the United States). Traffic was accommodated on a central carriage drive and meandering outer roads, allowing it to enter and exit without conflicting with visitors on foot. The plan of both parks emphasized a concern for pedestrian rather than vehicular traffic; Shaw had stated that his greatest concern was for those who would walk, rather than ride. Like Paxton, Shaw would provide walking paths that could be reached through ornamental gateways, anticipating that people might visit the park and botanical garden sequentially. Beside the need to accommodate such activities as "promenading" and mental relaxation, the increasing popularity of more active pastimes required ground reserved for group sports[10] (although incorporating large spaces for organized games and athletic exercises that often involved noise and large groups was a new concern for planners of the period). These first public parks were meant to provide a healthy alternative to less proper leisure activities; if one were out enjoying nature, and particularly if one were actively engaged in sports, there was less likelihood of inappropriate recreation such as overindulgence in drink.

A third similarity in terms of planning was to incorporate villas along the perimeter of the park.[11] The concept was to dedicate a percentage of park land to be sold as building lots, their lease or sale to provide funds for park maintenance. Shaw also hoped to build and lease villas that would generate income for the Mis-

souri Botanical Garden, and early maps of Tower Grove Park indicate lots in a two-hundred-foot strip lining the perimeter.[12] In
the end, the plan was unsuccessful, and Shaw built only one residence, an Italianate-style villa (1869) on Magnolia Avenue (it still
serves as the park director's house).

In addition to Paxton, Shaw looked once again to John Claudius
Loudon for ideas. The writings on horticulture and aesthetics
that had guided Shaw at the botanical garden, such as those in the
Encyclopedia of Gardening, manifested only part of Loudon's expertise. The subject of open spaces and alternating zones of town
and country around London had interested Loudon as early as
1829, as evidenced in his *Gardener's Magazine* article "Breathing
Places for the Metropolis," which was followed in 1835 by "Remarks on Laying out Public Parks and Promenades." In 1839 he
had accepted the commission to design the Derby Arboretum,
and his work there represented the culmination of his interest in
the creation of urban public spaces. In contrast to the arboretum
at Chatsworth, Derby was the first truly public park space created specifically for the enjoyment of all classes. The arboretum's
collection of 801 varieties of trees and shrubs, all identified by
markers, united "Information with Amusement," and provided
fresh air to citizens burdened by industrial growth.

The land for the Derby Arboretum was donated by a local
philanthropist and former mayor, Joseph Strutt. Increasingly in
the nineteenth century, the industrialist and the businessman replaced the aristocrat as benefactor, and this particular gift of private land for the public good very likely inspired Henry Shaw. On
September 16, 1840, the day the Derby Arboretum opened, Shaw
was traveling in Derbyshire between Birmingham and Sheffield,
and he may well have been in attendance (the Missouri Botanical
Garden Library owns a copy of the program provided at opening-
day celebrations).[13] His borrowing of ideas is evident in the simi-

lar mission of the two places: both Strutt and Shaw specifically defined the plans and use of space, emphasizing their concerns for public accessibility and the dual purpose of recreation and education.[14] Neither, though, provided an endowment for maintenance, a situation that would prove problematic in the future.[15]

Loudon's eighty-three-page *Plan of the Derby Arboretum* includes a planting plan, a map of the topography, and illustrations of its architecture—the Elizabethan-style main gate, a "James I" pavilion that marks the terminus of a crosswalk, and gatehouses. A catalogue of trees and shrubs and the opening-day remarks by the town council and Joseph Strutt are also included. Shaw's plan for Tower Grove Park, which he wrote in the late 1860s or early 1870s, has striking similarities to the Derby guide, although Shaw pays greater attention to aesthetics and to the actual experience of a park visit. When comparing the two documents one appreciates how closely Shaw follows Loudon's lead. Both planners address practicality and design concerns, then describe the landscape and location, the soil ("loamy" in each instance), and drainage. Physical description of the site is followed by statement of the primary purpose of the park. According to Loudon, the arboretum is a

The Elizabethan-style main entrance to Derby Arboretum.
From Loudon's Plan of the Derby Arboretum.

"To Unite Utility, Variety and Beauty"

"place of recreation for the inhabitants of Derby and the neighborhood, and for all other persons who choose to come see it." Shaw echoes this idea: "A public park should be so plann'd as to afford recreation to the greatest number."

Management, maintenance, and the mission of the park are each dealt with in separate sections by both Loudon and Shaw. The Derby Arboretum is to be overseen by a curator who occupies the north lodge; the responsibilities of gardeners are outlined (down to the removal of "worm-casts" and anthills), and the guide anticipates expenses involved in the process. Shaw specifies the main responsibility of his gardeners and laborers to be the trees, grass, and shrubbery—"the chief adornments" of the park—and keeping them in "order & good trim," and he notes the need for a minimum of $25,000 annually for maintenance, an amount that "will barely pay Superintendent, Gate keepers, Park Police, Gardeners, Laborers," and for annual painting. Where Shaw coincides most closely with Loudon is in discussion of the mission of the park beyond recreation. In keeping with the Victorian interest in education and improvement, these new public spaces are meant to provide both moral and practical education for the visitor. Derby's central purpose is "to excite an interest in the subject of trees and shrubs in the minds of general observers."[16] Strutt reiterates this mission on opening day, noting that the purpose of the improvements—the collection of trees and shrubs "laid out in the advantageous manner"—is to instruct and entertain.[17] Shaw confirms the same intent, to "interest the public in the knowledge of arboriculture"[18] by using the gardenesque method and uniting the useful and the beautiful.

Shaw's Aesthetics: Nature and Art

Shaw's decision about the aesthetics of Tower Grove Park is best understood against the backdrop of a long-standing discussion, especially in England, on the concept of the picturesque. His familiarity with the idea derives from the late-eighteenth-century debate in Britain that defined the subject,[19] and through his readings and his observation, especially during his travels, he came to understand what the picturesque looked like, and the moods it evoked. Beside the work of John Ruskin, the art critic who taught readers to contemplate the picturesque in both art and nature, Shaw owned the writings of two other British theorists who helped to define the subject, William Gilpin and Uvedale Price. The term, first used in Gilpin's *Observations Relative Chiefly to Picturesque Beauty* (1776), began as a reference to a view or object suitable for framing.[20] It was added to two aesthetic categories, the sublime and the beautiful, that had been defined in 1757 by Edmund Burke. Although its primary relation was to painting (and vision), the concept would be applied in other arts—architecture, literature, and landscape. The earliest discussions identified the picturesque as an aesthetic counterpart to untamed ephemeral nature, to wildness that appeared not to have met with the hand of man; but it would come to be understood in a broader sense as the discussion unfolded.

A concept of beauty defined by theorists in didactic poetry and essays, and a movement of taste rather than a precise style, the picturesque contrasted with established perceptions of the beautiful (that which is small, smooth, and soft) and the sublime (the vast, obscure, and terrifying).[21] This new third category was characterized by variety, irregularity, roughness, intricacy, and movement (also, surprise and anticipation). Such characteristic elements could be arranged in any number of ways and be inherent in a variety of objects: shaggy ponies, mossy crags, rushing water, filtered sunlight. In picturesque imagery, objects and compositions are various, flickering, uneven. When assembled in the viewer's mind they create an image of varied surfaces, textures, intricacies of light and color (and sound). As a mental construct, the picturesque is a composition, a picture or a series of pictures, drawn from nature.

As a "mode of vision," a "way of seeing," the picturesque emphasized pictorial values that could be used as tools for analyzing nature. More than a set of discrete characteristics, the picturesque was understood as a sensibility that could be perfected by the act of looking. Once one could appreciate the picturesque in paintings (the artists Claude Lorrain and Salvator Rosa were cited as examples to study) one could appreciate it in nature. The British theorist Uvedale Price, whom Shaw cites among his list of influences, contributed to the definition of the aesthetic in his *Essay on the Picturesque* (1794), in which he was precise and clear about how elements such as water, trees, grass, curves, and distances should be "disposed" in order to be picturesque.[22] Friend and fellow theorist Richard Payne Knight responded the same year with a didactic poem, *The Landscape*, a dialogue on landscape aesthetics that advocated irregularity and complexity, and identified the proper ingredients for correct picturesque effects.[23] Picturesque theory became explicit in William Gilpin's guidebooks, including *Observations on the River Wye* (1782) and the *Lake District* (1789). Having read Gilpin, one could travel to the region equipped with the proper sensibilities and record knobby tree trunks, gnarled roots, and rocky outcroppings by drawing, painting, or writing.

By 1820 the aesthetic had made its way to America, and for the next fifty years it would be widely applied to American sensibilities and landscape. The meaning of the picturesque was learned, altered, and adapted to suit a democratic country in the process of refinement.[24] It framed the discussion of a range of topics including art and literature, and in the writings of Emerson and Thoreau the picturesque embodied the spiritual. In America as in Britain, it was accessible and easily adapted, by the common as well as the refined citizen, and it cut across geographic boundaries as well. By the mid- to late nineteenth century it had become the status quo—a way of seeing the country and appreciating it in both visual and written form.

Timing contributed to the success of the picturesque in America. When it arrived, the country was in the process of reshaping its national mission and identity. Landscape, both actual and in the form of paintings by Thomas Cole, Asher B. Durand, and the Hudson River School, became the expression of progress and of manifest destiny. When these artists painted the creeks and rocks[25] of the Catskills and the White Mountains their intention was more than to create picturesque representations of water and woods; their work commented on difficult themes that plagued the country—its present and future, spirituality, racial harmony, and the process of nation building. Yet landscape also represented values, in particular, aesthetic values. Through nature, and the picturesque handling of it, Americans not only learned about themselves and their country, they learned about art.

American appreciation of these matters culminated in the publication of William Cullen Bryant's two-volume *Picturesque America* (1874), an epic tour of the country's celebrated places, its life, and its habits. Publications such as Appleton's *Illustrated Handbook of American Travel* (1857) and their *Railway and Steam Navigation Guide* (1869) had facilitated travel in America, but for average citizens it was not just practicality that compelled them to tour nearby landscapes. For most, the country ramble trumped the Grand Tour in terms of aesthetics.[26] Local scenery captivated the public imagination, and it was perceived in picturesque terms (later in the century, travel to the Far West would introduce the sublime as an alternative expression). From the writings of A. J. Downing, citizens learned to apply aesthetics—both the beautiful and the picturesque—to their own landscapes. Thus Americans were educated to appreciate the beautiful in the common and everyday, and the picturesque came to express quality of life and civic responsibility; understanding it was the mark of a literate citizen. Education and improvement, two prime objectives of the period, were thus facilitated by an appreciation of aesthetics.

Henry Shaw understood the picturesque as an aesthetic and its power to teach and communicate. On his travels in England

and Wales in the 1840s, he had participated in the fashionable activity of touring the countryside, visiting the scenic village of Matlock (Derbyshire), known for its mountainous terrain, cascades, and the winding river Derwent with its gorge.[27] There he had, in Gilpin's words, felt "the imagination take fire." Shaw's sensitivity is clear in his description of Tower Grove Park, as he evokes for the viewer the experience of the place. He takes us on a stroll through the park, passing bridges, ornamental seats, and the evergreen walk, someday to be "shady and agreeable." He characterizes trees as "spiral Norways," "lofty Poplars," and "scarlet Oaks," elaborating on their varied placement and effect: "The trees have been placed with reference to shade in lines, groups, and single, and with regard to verdant tints and autumn colors . . . someday [they] will have a fine effect for the groups are so arranged that the light and dark tints will afford agreeable contrast."[28] Shaw composes the scene with the eye of an artist, admiring variety of effect in the placement of trees, envisioning a broken, irregular play of light and shadow in autumn (defined by advocates as the most picturesque of seasons). His ability to view the whole in pictorial terms, his capacity to think and see in a picturesque way, is clear.

In spite of his appreciation for the picturesque, however, Shaw would choose a very different aesthetic for the plan of Tower Grove Park. His reasoning reflects his hybrid personality, rooted in two centuries and two countries. His decision reveals his determination to leave a personal mark on Tower Grove and on St. Louis, and his desire to educate the public through "garden botany."

In the December 1832 *Gardener's Magazine* editor John Claudius Loudon had professed the importance of going beyond established concepts and methods, announcing that "mere picturesque improvement is not enough in these enlightened times: it is necessary to understand that there is such a character as the gardenesque."[29] Loudon was building on existing picturesque theories of beauty that had been adopted by landscape advocates such as Humphry Repton, who had sensed change in the world of gardening and taste and believed that the two would increasingly be dictated by the middle class rather than by the elite. And soon the introduction and display of newly identified species and varieties from around the world stimulated interest in plants as subject matter. Loudon followed in Repton's footsteps when he called for a change in the way grounds were laid out and planted[30] in order to accommodate the growing interest in garden botany. As a response to this need for appropriate methods of display Loudon defined the "gardenesque."

The gardenesque—not a style but a method of planting and display—dictated that plants, shrubs, and trees be treated individually, as specimens. Discrete placement allowed specimens to grow to full capacity without crowding and thus develop their natural characteristics completely. Often they were arranged according to type and dimension and then thinned out as needed to create enough space to make natural form and habit clearly visible. By definition, this method of separation and control made each plant a unique botanical statement. This museum-like approach, showcasing plants like freestanding sculpture, heightened the reference to art. Loudon believed also that the use of exotic plants, rather than those that could be found in the surrounding landscape, would best communicate to viewers that gardens were works of art rather than nature. In both respects—the showcasing of individual specimens and the reference to art—the gardenesque was the antithesis of the picturesque aesthetic, in which variety, irregularity, and massed groupings crowded together blurred the boundaries between the park or garden and nature at large. Loudon explained to readers of *The Encyclopedia of Gardening*:

> To understand the difference between these styles, it must be observed that the picturesque style [is known] by that irregularity in

Giant century plant displayed as sculpture at Tower Grove Park.

forms, lines, and general composition which we see in natural landscape, while in the gardenesque style all the trees, shrubs, and plants are planted and managed in such a way that each may arrive at its highest state of individual perfection, and display its beauties to as great advantage as if it were cultivated for that purpose alone, while, at the same time, the plants relatively to one another, and to the whole scene or place to which they belong, are placed regularly and systematically.[31]

Loudon illustrated the contrast between the two in his 1838 book *The Suburban Gardener, and Villa Companion.*

View of the gardenesque plantings from the roof of the superintendant's house at Tower Grove Park.

The gardenesque emphasis on specimens as subject matter made the choice of plants critical. Not only were plants used to create the environment and mood of a place, they were tools for learning. In general, trees and shrubs were valued over flowers as the defining elements of gardenesque parks. Although there was some agreement that a "blaze" of flowers was an effective means of capturing the attention of the uneducated (thereby providing the opportunity for instruction), contemporary writers suggested that worthy parks should comprise impressive collections of trees and shrubs, with flowers limited to specific areas such as entrances and junctions of pathways. In arboreta, flower gardens were rarely incorporated, or were considered as objects "detached and distinct from the general scenery of the place."[32] Critics considered the improper use of flowers an assault to the sensibilities; unnecessary, frivolous additions interfered with the serious mission of a public park.[33] Instead of a scattering of flower beds, parks were more often ornamented with large vases filled with New Zealand flax or century plants (agave), or pots filled with new introductions chosen for their unusual shape, foliage, vivid color, and often large size (as in the case of banana plants and bamboo).

The gardenesque was a fashionable method that implied, if not the refined sensibilities of a garden's owner or a park's visitors, the fact that they were up-to-date, informed. Appreciation of this method reflected social, financial, and class distinctions—tearing up one's garden and replanting it in the gardenesque mode could be labor-intensive and expensive. It was used alongside other popular methods of planting, such as carpet bedding and massing, where thousands of identical greenhouse-raised annuals, or collections of cacti or sedum, were placed in single beds (one Loudon protégé, Edward Kemp, used the term "mixed style" to suggest this combination of various types of planting within an overall composition). It was not so much the number of items on one's plant list but the rarity of specimens from all over the world that displayed one's wealth. Gardens have always conveyed the status of their owners as enlightened, informed, and sometimes wealthy individuals; the gardenesque also communicated intellectual sophistication—participation in the new avocation of garden botany and awareness of the aesthetic debate, as published in new horticultural journals, that dictated method.

Loudon's work permitted viewers to appreciate the specific characteristics of a plant, yet maintained the composition and unity of expression necessary in designed landscapes. In the hands of less judicious practitioners, however, the gardenesque came to be synonymous with an "aesthetic of scatter."[34] Critics felt the effect similar to that of an explosion in a greenhouse, its contents landing randomly across a lawn; a lack of cohesion in overall design was the most important failing of the method, an overabundance of ornamental effects another. Those opposed to Loudon's method considered it to be excessive, resulting in a garden layout characterized by "rampant eclecticism and lack of artistic unity."[35] These criticisms, along with a growing interest in the use of native rather than exotic plants and changes in taste—in particular, an aesthetic preference for pastoral effects—would put an end to the use of the gardenesque method by the third quarter of the nineteenth century.

Henry Shaw weighed which aesthetic, the picturesque or the gardenesque, was most appropriate for Tower Grove Park. The different principles and visual effects of each were clear from his readings, and his writings confirm his understanding of the two. In his written plan he dismisses the picturesque as a style best suited to landscape painting, insisting that "wild nature" is not the intention of the landscape gardener. Concurring with Loudon that the gardenesque is the ideal approach for improvement in the countryside because it most forcibly contrasts with the surrounding scenery,[36] he chose "the cultivated or gardenesque style" for Tower Grove Park. Shaw's choice appealed to those with a taste for botany, and addressed social concerns via an aesthetic method. Its display of trees and plants created a "living museum" that effectively facilitated learning, and thereby fulfilled one of the park's main purposes—to provide intellectual stimulation, to educate and improve. By using the gardenesque Shaw had chosen not to "outrage" nature with "abrupt curves or distorted forms," but instead unite "utility, variety and beauty."[37]

Shaw's choice of the gardenesque reflects two important changes in the American public that were becoming clear. First, the middle classes—the citizens of St. Louis—were increasingly fluent in aesthetics; ideas about beauty were no longer an elitist monopoly. That aesthetics could contribute to intellectual development, moral sensibility, and refinement of taste was a topic of public discussion in publications such as *The American Woman's Home*.[38] Second, the distinction between art and nature was taking on new importance in a country more visually literate than ever before. Those not yet sensitized to matters of taste were becoming so by reading the many publications featuring the subject and by seeing examples in the landscape. The idea that the picturesque evoked nature and the gardenesque evoked art was one the viewing public could increasingly appreciate, and a distinction the park's board of commissioners clearly understood.

His rejection of the picturesque placed Shaw at odds with other landscape enthusiasts. A. J. Downing, for example, who had ardently promoted the picturesque, advocated the concept of a "national" landscape that artistically coincided with a "natural" one.[39] Likewise, the aesthetic choice of Olmsted and Vaux at Central Park mimicked nature and was clearly a picturesque handling of it.[40] Shaw appreciated the approach championed by these park planners, but he believed (from his readings) that the application of a given aesthetic was dependent on the situation and that "in matters of taste opinions are various." That the gardenesque was at odds with a different and increasingly mainstream expression was of little consequence to him.

Shaw's choice also reflected changing contemporary notions about nature itself. Beginning as an aesthetic expression but expanding to represent national identity and democratic ideals, the picturesque had always implied a strong connection to nature, and mossy banks, fractured sunlight, and rippled pools of water often implied references to spirituality. The Transcendentalist thought of Emerson and Thoreau, for example, fused nature and religion often through picturesque imagery. But Darwin's *On the Origin of Species* in 1859 (the year Shaw opened his garden to the public) challenged ideas of the divinity of nature and rocked established notions that nature and God were one. After Darwin, many began to view nature as a scientific phenomenon rather than the creation of a higher power; some botanists, geologists, and naturalists responded by divorcing science from religion in order to justify faith. Shaw believed that planting trees and flowers was more valuable work than ministry,[41] and so the gardenesque, with its ties to the science of botany, proved more appealing than the picturesque, with its ties to the spiritual.

Shaw's decision to employ the gardenesque also involved his concern for propriety—his sense of what an appropriately designed *American* landscape should be and what it should look like. He knew to avoid the stiffness of formal order, "the geometric style" he had seen in Europe at Versailles, for example; his was a public park, not royal grounds. On the other hand, Shaw's interest in the role of art in landscape gardening dictated that not only should the hand of man be visible, there should be clearly identifiable "artistic conceptions and arrangements."[42] Evidence of creative intervention echoed Loudon's remark that no gentleman would be flattered by having his grounds mistaken for uncultivated countryside.[43] The 1883 report on Tower Grove Park, written by Shaw's friend David MacAdam, often used Shaw's words verbatim, and he explained Shaw's choice in this way: "The artist of the graceful and cultivated style pursues, then, a middle course between the picturesque and the formality of the purely artificial, aiming always to preserve the harmony of natural forms and scenes."[44] When first defined in the eighteenth century, the picturesque was itself an aesthetic expression set between polar opposites—the sublime and the beautiful. As originally defined by Loudon, the gardenesque was an improvement on the picturesque, and one that the enlightened nineteenth century demanded. Shaw viewed the gardenesque as a nineteenth-century improvement on ideas of beauty, the midpoint between the picturesque and the formal style.

This middle course seems an appropriate choice for the American landscape, particularly a midwestern one. In the spirit of A. J. Downing, who maintained that good taste was modest taste, it suggests moderation and suitability, a visual and practical solution to planning that represents the greatest number and communicates shared values.[45] The fact, however, that Shaw's middle choice was the gardenesque is difficult for today's audience to comprehend—it seems excessive, not representative of American values or aesthetics. In general, we accept the prairie or majestic mountains to be a more appropriate American expression. But Shaw's judgment was shaped by his circumstances and experience: he was a complex mix of eighteenth-century sensibilities and nineteenth-century interests—a self-made man who shared his fortune and intellect by enlightening the public; a man born in industrial England who chose to live in the American Midwest; a gentleman who held close to his heart both a memory of England and the future of America. Shaw carried out his "own plan and design," believing he "had sufficient reasons for doing so."[46] To him the prairie represented opportunity and sovereignty, but not artistic expression; it represented a starting point, a landscape waiting to be improved. Although Shaw's choice of the gardenesque seems extravagant through the lens of history, it was at that time and to him the best choice—harmonious and without extreme, a middle course that represented the middle class.

Use, Education, and Matters of Taste

Shaw described his intentions in a handwritten, ten-page proposal titled "The Plan of the Park and Reasons for Its Adoption."[47] Its seven parts, organized by topic, address practical matters such as drainage, maintenance, and staff, as well as aesthetic concerns such as beauty and taste.[48] Shaw begins by identifying his main objective: to create ornamental improvements that suit the purpose and provide recreation to the greatest number. Shaw's vision, and the plan's scope, is not limited to the park proper. He notes planting trees (two hundred of them in 1870) to beautify the neighborhood surrounding the park. He also suggests planting them "in Boulevard Style," to ornament main avenues that radiate from the city center and link neighborhoods.[49] This idea anticipates improvements made decades later as a response to the city's 1891 Boulevard Law, and the City Beautiful movement in general.[50] One of the main points of Shaw's plan deals with theories of beauty as they relate to planning and reflects the park's twin missions of recreation and education.

Shaw's discussion of aesthetics, or what he calls "matters of taste," begins with three sets of influences that frame his thinking. He lists them as

1st My experience in the formation of the Botanical Gardens & arboretum at Tower Grove—

2nd The public parks and promenades I have visited in England, France, Germany, Spain, Portugal, Italy & other countries—

3rd From reading eminent authors on Landscape Gardening—Sir Uvedale Price on the pictoresque [*sic*]—Repton—Gilpin—Loudon—Downing etc.[51]

Shaw had visited the major parks of France, Germany, and Spain, as well as royal grounds as far east as Russia, and he credits them as an influence on his sensibilities. But he was critically aware of the preeminence of the British as innovators in the field of aesthetics since the landscape movement of the eighteenth century. He knew that Europe looked to England for direction, and that in France, Italy, and Germany existing gardens had been torn up and replanted to replicate the fashionable English style, evident in the profusion of the *jardin anglais*, *giardino inglese*, and *Englischer Garten* across Europe.[52] Third, Shaw's list of "eminent authors" reads like a history of the subject: Price and Gilpin as definers of the picturesque; Humphry Repton, the first person to call himself a "landscape gardener"; Loudon, Shaw's primary source for horticultural improvement; and A. J. Downing, America's proponent of good taste in the landscape. Close at hand, on Shaw's library shelf, theory and practical information came from all the books and encyclopedias, and in the newest mode of communication, horticultural journals, to which he subscribed.[53]

Shaw added two penciled citations, between the lines and in the margin, to this list of primary and secondary sources. These were "the annual reports of the New York Parks and Alfords [*sic*] Parks and promenades of Paris." Here he acknowledges the report of two recent projects in New York, Manhattan's Central

Park (1858) and Prospect Park in Brooklyn (1867), although he never mentions their designers, Frederick Law Olmsted and Calvert Vaux, by name (the only comments Shaw ever made regarding these parks refer to size and budget).[54] His second marginal addition cites a recent two-volume work, *Les promenades de Paris*, written between 1867 and 1873 by Jean Charles Adolphe Alphand, the *jardinier-ingénieur* (garden engineer) to Baron Haussmann, who rebuilt much of Paris under Napoleon III in the years 1853–69. Alphand was responsible for reworking Paris's Bois de Boulogne from a private hunting ground to a public space that emulated London's Hyde Park, acknowledging contemporary British innovations in park planning.[55] He also designed the much smaller Parc Monceau (Shaw's favorite of the two).

Drawing on Paxton's experiments at the Chatsworth arboretum, Shaw emphasizes the important role played by deciduous trees, conifers, and evergreens, for their educational interest and for their ability to convey abstract concepts. He indicates that trees, grass, and shrubbery are the chief adornments of the park. No flower beds are provided for in the original design, although huge exotics in decorative pots, appreciated as distinctively different from flowers as ornaments, were used. Shaw writes that "flower Gardening can form no part of our work," pointing out the expense and added maintenance of flowers. He notes that their beauty can be enjoyed in separate surroundings, close by at the botanical garden, a comment confirming that he viewed park and garden as separate, yet complementary, entities, each with its own characteristics, including aesthetic impression and function.[56]

Just as A. J. Downing equated the power and majesty of trees with the rights of the individual, Shaw acknowledged that they were ideal for public exhibition. Traditionally valued for their civilizing effect on society, and as metaphors for liberty, strength, and national identity, trees were no longer elite symbols but increasingly viewed as icons of democratic ideals. Their "commanding attitude" in a public park communicated a defining characteristic of these new places—a sense of ownership.[57] Because Shaw's park, and the prototypes he referred to, were created specifically for the working man and his family, they were, by definition, inclusive: trees, once solely the possession of the wealthy, became accessible to all, and public parks became representative of equality, and in America, democracy.

An entire section of Shaw's plan deals with the care of trees—arboriculture—and includes a list of those he intends to plant at the park. He cites twenty-seven deciduous trees, evergreens, and conifers—although this amount increases dramatically once planting is complete—all to be labeled with their proper botanical names (inspected for correctness by George Engelmann). In addition to native trees, "the hardiest and healthiest kinds," exotic species were planted from Europe and Asia, although Shaw's interest in a varied collection that reflects connoisseurship is balanced by the practical concerns of a horticulturist. "The finest and best trees adapted to the soil and climate of Missouri," many from northern Europe, Siberia, China and Japan, were used in greater number than imports "introduced to science in the last fifty years" from Australia, Southern Africa, Northern India, and South America. The araucarias (including the monkey puzzle tree so popular in England), eucalyptus, cedars of Lebanon and India, so prized in Europe, had been tried but failed (except as greenhouse plants) through inability to withstand the harsh Missouri climate. In collecting trees Shaw ultimately chose a pragmatic (and environmentally sensible) approach, planting those best suited to the region.

Constructing and Ornamenting Tower Grove Park

In October 1868, Shaw had gained the city's approval to move forward with park plans, and his donation of nearly three hundred acres of land was finalized. Now signing his name as "Comptroller" of the park, he began a detailed list of infrastructure and improvements, a "Synopsis of Work Done." Subsequently, a record of costs would be submitted to city officials in annual reports. Francis Tunica, who had worked with Shaw at the garden and drawn one of the finest plans depicting garden, arboretum, and fruticetum, was hired as supervisor of construction based on his qualifications as engineer and architect. He had lived in St. Louis for fifteen years, served on the Lafayette Park committee, and won six design commissions in the city. Now Tunica would direct the frenzy of construction activity at Tower Grove Park, first designing and building the superintendent's house and then implementing Shaw's plan over the next three years, until the completion of the park.

In January 1869, Shaw and Tunica toured the perimeter to assess progress. Bounded on four sides by Grand Avenue (east), Kingshighway (west), Magnolia Avenue (north), and Arsenal Street (south), the park consisted of an oblong strip of land, one and a third miles long and a quarter mile wide, situated south of and perpendicular to the garden. Drives, walks, and

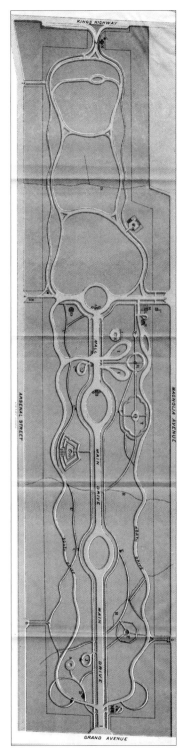

The plan of Tower Grove Park, from David MacAdam's publication of 1883.

The western meadow.

Photo by Carol Betsch.

bridges would not be completed until 1871, but Shaw had determined their location. The eastern length of the park would be bisected by a processional central drive with occasional "turnouts" accompanied by meandering secondary circuit walks of brick, gravel, and grass. In contrast, the western portion would consist of an unbroken meadow (and accompanying views) framed by pedestrian walks along the perimeter. Plowing and cultivating of soil, and sowing of blue grass and timothy on

View into the meadow.
Photo by Carol Betsch.

Pedestrian bridge.
Photo by Carol Betsch.

Tower Grove Park   133

Pedestrian path.

Photo by Carol Betsch.

*Trees bordering
a walkway.*

Photo by Carol Betsch.

approximately 150 acres was complete. An initial 250 loads of stone were used for drains and wells. The plan called for ten bridges of iron, stone, and wood, variously ornamented, to cross shallow watercourses. Over 35,000 feet of walks were to be macadamized and graveled, and another 5,000 feet of grass walks were under way; nearly 16,000 feet of drives, some 45 feet wide, were lined with stone guttering. A total of seven miles of circulation routes would accommodate those on horseback, in

View along a drive.

Photo by Carol Betsch.

vehicles, and on foot. Pedestrian gates led to walks that enabled visitors to proceed from one end of the park to the other without the necessity of crossing over carriageways. The monumental east (main) gate on Grand Avenue, the west gate (visually similar to several of Loudon's plans), and the north gate—with columns from the Old Courthouse—all designed by Tunica, were constructed. A 19,500-foot hedge of American arbor vitae,

The Bull Pen pedestrian gate on Magnolia Avenue.

Photo by Carol Betsch.

"To Unite Utility, Variety and Beauty"

*The Maury
pedestrian gate on
Arsenal Street.*
Photo by Carol Betsch.

*Walkway inside the
Maury Gate.*
Photo by Carol Betsch.

Henry Shaw in his carriage at the Grand Avenue entrance to the park.

The Loudonesque west gate on Kingshighway.

backed by a cedar and pine fence, was planted to surround the perimeter.[58]

Planting had begun; the list of twenty-seven species of trees Shaw had listed in his "Plan of the Park" was only an initial estimate, and the amount increased dramatically. The February 1869 order to the F. K. Phoenix company, which had supplied plants for the garden, listed nearly 9,000 trees and shrubs. The second annual report of Tower Grove Park listed (as of December 1870),

17,119 specimens of 104 different varieties of trees, shrubs, and vines in the nurseries of Tower Grove Park and the botanical garden, ready and awaiting planting the following year. The inventory indicates the botanical and popular names and the number of each ready to plant; it also suggests the arrangement followed in planting them.[59] For example, hundreds of the spruce, pine, and cedar trees became the park's elliptical Evergreen Walk and the Evergreen Circle; 722 hemlock and 1,204 Norway spruce

North gate entrance.

Photo by Carol Betsch.

were arranged into a labyrinth (with walks 12 to 14 feet wide), based on the maze at Hampton Court, England;[60] five varieties of *Fraxinus*—ash trees—were grouped to facilitate comparison; and scarlet flowering trumpet vine and red coral honeysuckle ornamented the summerhouse of the Children's Playground.

Many of the deciduous trees in the inventory were Missouri natives: maples (1,670 "white" maples alone were used), oaks, birch, ash, and buckeyes. Shrubs included mock orange, callicarpa, St. John's wort, kalmia, and weigela; the ornamental trees ready for planting were five species of magnolia (172 of three varieties possibly grouped together), flowering crabapples, and ginkgo. Varieties not native to Missouri included lime trees (*Tilia europaea*), mahonia, six *Halesia tetraptera* ("snowdrop tree"), and twelve "tree cranberries." According to Shaw's directions, trees would be planted as specimens along drives and walks, and arranged in groups (and as specimens) throughout; each would be planted in a space dug five feet wide and three feet deep, and then staked and tied (and later, labeled).

Drawing of the labyrinth, ca. 1875.

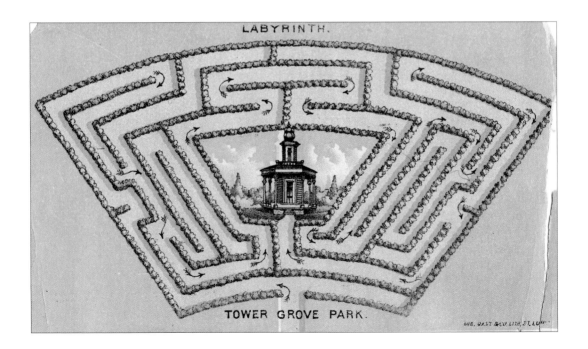

After the main planting and the building of infrastructure, a team of architects, engineers, stonemasons, carpenters, and gardeners worked in 1871–73 to construct Tower Grove Park's twelve colorful and ornate pavilions (or "summerhouses," as Shaw called them), gatehouses, and a sailboat pond accented with mock ruins made with recycled stone from the Lindell Hotel fire of 1867. Additional buildings would be added until 1888. The eclectic mixing of architectural styles that was popular during the nineteenth century is apparent throughout the park, in Gothic and Romanesque Revival structures, Flemish gables, picturesque rockwork, and polychrome gazebos.

Francis Tunica, who had gained skills working with the U.S. Engineers Bureau during the Civil War, had graded, guttered, and laid out the site, and as supervisor oversaw the initial phase of construction. Besides the superintendent's house, Tunica is credited with designing the stable complex and the three gates and gatehouses on the park's perimeter. Shaw's friend the London-trained architect George Barnett, who had designed

Sons of Rest Pavilion, ca. 1878.

Old Playground Pavilion.

Photo by Carol Betsch.

View to the Carriage Pavilion.

Photo by Carol Betsch.

Sailboat pond and
mock ruins, ca. 1880.

The pond and ruins
in early morning.
Photo by Carol Betsch.

his town house and the Italianate villa at the garden in 1849, as well as an arbor for his private gardens, for the park designed a palm house in 1878 (in collaboration with his associate, Issac Taylor) and another virtually identical one in 1885 (now known as the Piper Palm House and Piper Plant House, respectively).[61] Both bear a strong resemblance to the Nash Conservatory at Kew (and to their sister palm house, the Linnean House, at the botanical garden). Barnett was responsible for the south gate

Kingshighway gatehouse.

Photo by Carol Betsch.

South entrance gatehouse, Arsenal Street.

Photo by Carol Betsch.

Music Stand,
ca. 1878.

View of the Turkish
Pavilion.

Photo by Carol Betsch.

and the South Lodge, the last major construction at the park in 1888, a year before Shaw's death.[62]

Little is known about two other figures involved with the architecture of Tower Grove Park. Eugene Greenleaf, architect, designer, or draftsman, was responsible for many of the important park structures built in 1871–72. The Music Stand and the Turkish Pavilion[63]—two of the most flamboyant pavilions centrally located in the park—are credited to Greenleaf, as is the

View of the Chinese Pavilion.

Photo by Carol Betsch.

Sons of Rest summerhouse and decorative elements such as well houses and the children's playground. He was listed in city directories alternately as a carpenter or architect and builder and his office was near that of Tunica and Barnett. Even less is known of Henry Thiele, who worked on park projects between 1872 and 1875 and may have been the draftsman responsible for large drawn plans of the park that indicate specific tree types and placement. Thiele is credited with designing the Chinese Pavilion and the carriage stand, built for parking vehicles and for use as a horse shade. Receipts and vouchers reveal the names of contractors, builders, and suppliers, and amounts paid for work done, but most of the craftsmen and laborers who constructed and planted the park remain anonymous. Records from 1870 indicate the total number of workmen employed ranged from 19 in the month of January to 165 in April, at a cost of nearly $60,000. These included painters, stonemasons, cutters and carpenters, foremen, teamsters, and drivers for carts and a two-horse wagon and plow. During 1870 only one gardener was employed (two in the months of November and December), suggesting that most of the work was done by laborers under the direction of James Gurney, head gardener and supervisor of the garden who for several years oversaw planting at both garden and park.

A "Gem of Sparkling Beauty"

Tower Grove Park opened officially on September 28, 1872. From the beginning, Sundays and holidays such as July 4 were the busiest days. The "throngs of visitors" Shaw had anticipated came to enjoy concerts, to celebrate the installation of the heroic bronze statues of Christopher Columbus, William Shakespeare, and Alexander von Humboldt that he had commissioned (which were cast at the Royal Bronze Foundry in Munich), or to enjoy the camaraderie of various fraternal and religious organizations

Visitors in Tower Grove Park, ca. 1876.

Alexander von Humboldt statue, ca. 1890.

Park trees in late afternoon.

Photo by Carol Betsch.

that met there. Contemporaries called the park "a gem of sparkling beauty," filled with bowers and vine-clad trellises, accented with artistic bridges, pagodas, and fountains.[64] Visitors slipped in through pedestrian gates to stroll the "shady and agreeable" Evergreen Walk, or "ramble through the pleasant scenes, making detours to the right or left as occasion may require."[65] Those "taxed and wearied by metropolitan life" could rest; others could take in the exhibition of evergreens, deciduous trees, and

Silver maples.

Photo by Carol Betsch.

shrubs, a composition of nature and art, where labeled specimens transformed looking into learning.

On Sunday, June 23, 1878, six years after it opened, Shaw recorded the number of visitors and their means of entry. From the east gate (the gate closest to the city limits) 683 carriages entered, as did fifteen saddle horses. Through the west gate passed 383 carriages and thirteen saddle horses, and from the north gate 246 carriages and one horse and rider. Four hundred one pedestrians came to visit that particular Sunday, for a total of 1,741 in attendance. Numbers were increasing annually. Additions to the park prompted return visits and rise in attendance, as, for example, when the first palm house was completed in 1878. The palm house remained open to the public in all seasons as a refuge for parties caught in showers or windy weather, though its primary function was to provide winter protection for exotic, nonhardy

Music Stand.

Photo by Carol Betsch.

foliage plants, ornamentals, and potted trees. The first winter it housed 343 palms, agaves, yuccas, and orange trees; these and others were set out in tubs and decorative boxes each summer, their botanical labels a "source of instruction and pleasure to the enquiring visitors."[66]

Cultural events, in particular music programs, attracted a great number of visitors. Summer concerts featuring the St. Louis Grand Orchestra, local bands, and German singing societies were presented under the festive and colorful backdrop of the Music Stand. A flamboyant octagonal pavilion with an onion dome topped with orb and spire, it is ornamented with multicolor scrolled brackets, wooden pendants, and carved moldings. The pattern of its elaborate cast-iron railings is echoed in nearby footbridges. This fantastic Orientalist stage, set against park greenery, is the social hub of the park. Originally it was shaded by striped awnings and surrounded by moon-shaped flower beds with urns of dramatic plants set among the rows of seating.

Music Stand, ca. 1890 (with redesigned roof for better acoustics).
Courtesy State Historical Society of Missouri, Columbia.

Tower Grove Park   **153**

Groupings of ginkgo, tulip, and Osage orange trees screen the circular walk. On July 6, 1884, as on many other occasions, Shaw celebrated the things he loved—music, art, summer evenings in the park. The newest addition to the park was a series of sculpted marble busts of his favorite composers Shaw was arranging to circle the Music Stand. The special event that July evening was the unveiling of Wagner and Beethoven, who were joining Rossini and Mozart (Gounod and Verdi would follow two years later). The weather was warm, the crowd appreciative, and the program, outstanding.

4

"Beauty, Instructiveness & Adaptability to Research"

THE EVOLUTION OF PARK AND GARDEN

Arboriculture and park keeping can never stand still, . . . with the practice of economy and the avoidance of costly ornamentation, of short durability and often of doubtful taste; . . . [the goal is] to plant and sow, that we or our successors may reap and gather.
—HENRY SHAW, personal notes (January 1, 1878)

By the time Tower Grove Park opened Shaw was in his seventies. He spent less time returning to the city to dine with friends and more time enjoying concerts and exhibitions at the park and garden. He visited with those who stopped by to do the same: casual observers such as twenty members of the Democratic convention, and the botanists Joseph Dalton Hooker and Asa Gray on their way to a botanical expedition in Colorado. Shaw traveled a little himself in the last years of his life: he regularly left the 90-degree heat and 90-percent humidity of Missouri summers to visit cooler Wisconsin and Mackinac Island, Michigan. A few years earlier he, too, had gone to Colorado, taking with him his cousin Henry Hoole of Sheffield and Joseph Monell, a young man who had been orphaned during

Henry Shaw at 85,
1885.

the Civil War when his mother, a Shaw employee, died. Shaw had financed Monell's education, but Monell was more than his charge. He had grown to refer to Shaw as "Pa" and would write to him from his home in Mine la Motte, Missouri, about his new-born daughter, referring to her as "your little namesake."

But Shaw had always called his plants his children, and later in life he spent considerable time writing about two of his favorites. In 1879 he coauthored, with James Gurney, *The Rose*, a twenty-nine-page historical and descriptive booklet. In it he spoke poignantly of leaves "still fragrant" even though they had been gathered at Tower Grove years earlier, in 1852, just after his move to the country. At eighty-four years of age, about the time he gave up his favorite wine, claret, for health reasons, he wrote

The Vine and Civilization, seventy-one pages on the history of wine, or viniculture. He wrote that "the vine" represented the true hallmark of a given society, was inseparable from it, and that its quality and temperate use reflected the degree of sophistication of a civilization.

On July 6, 1884, as Shaw sat in the audience listening to the concert in Tower Grove Park, he no doubt felt assured and comfortable that his affairs were in order. With the help of Asa Gray, who had visited him in early summer, he was in the process of revising his will. This time he had sought Gray's advice not for his expertise as a botanist but for his "superior judgment" as a patriarch in the field, the "captain of botanical industry."[1] Having served as one of the regents of the Smithsonian Institution, Gray worked to promote the science of botany by acquainting those who influenced private and government spending with the requirements, and costs, of botanical investigation. Thus he could give Shaw good counsel on how to ensure a sound future for his garden and the new school of botany Shaw hoped to found at Washington University.

Gray recognized that Shaw's will provided grand opportunities for the botanical garden and guaranteed the development of the "Mississippian Kew."[2] Shaw's desire to establish a professorship in the name of his friend and colleague George Engelmann, who had died in February, would also be arranged. Other bequests outlined in the will reflected Shaw's concern for more modest, but no less significant, matters: he asked that there be a gardeners' banquet, a flower show, and a "Flower Sermon" at Christ Church Cathedral held annually in his memory. And in these last years, Shaw and Gray discussed more than garden business and the details of his will. Shaw confided to Gray that he dreaded the debilitating conditions of old age and implied a regret for his lack of a loving helpmate and companion.[3]

Shaw died at 3:25 a.m. on August 25, 1889, in his bedroom at Tower Grove, which overlooked the first gardens he had planted. Among those at his side were his sister Caroline, his devoted

Henry Shaw, holding a rose, lying in state, August 1889.

housekeeper Rebecca Edom, and James Gurney.[4] Mayor E. A. Noonan ordered flags to be flown at half-mast, and a period of mourning in the city. Shaw's body, in a casket surrounded by palms and draped with black velvet, lay in state at the garden museum to allow city fathers and the public to pay their respects. At the funeral at Christ Church Cathedral, Gurney would be asked to lead the pallbearers—all of them garden employees— down the Osage orange avenue, across the grounds, to Shaw's

final resting place, the granite mausoleum in the grove. On the tomb lay a marble sculpture of Shaw holding a rose.

Shaw's mausoleum.
Photo by Carol Betsch.

Shaw's death marked a major transition for the Missouri Botanical Garden and Tower Grove Park. The very hands-on Mr. Shaw, who had overseen all aspects of development, was replaced by trustees in the case of the garden, and his place on the Tower Grove Park board was, according to his will, filled by the garden's director. The position, at the suggestion of Asa Gray, would be filled by William Trelease, who was serving as the first Engelmann Professor at the Shaw School of Botany, Washington University.[5] James Gurney, the Royal Botanic Society–trained gardener who had worked alongside Shaw since 1867, continued in the role of superintendent of Tower Grove Park. During Trelease's and Gurney's tenures a new century would begin and new priorities would be established; taste and circumstance would dictate a change in aesthetics and, ultimately, modifications to Shaw's park and botanical garden.

William Trelease in the office at Tower Grove House, December 1, 1889.

"Beauty, Instructiveness & Adaptability to Research"

For the most part, Tower Grove Park remained as Shaw had last visited it. It continued to be used for Sunday and holiday concerts and for cultural and educational events. The need for more funding for labor and maintenance, a problem Shaw had anticipated in 1871, began to strain the budget and sparked a debate between city officials and the garden board which lasted for decades.[6] What changed the most at Tower Grove Park after Shaw's death was the nature, and extent, of the park's ornamentation: more color, greater abundance, and new decorative installations to satisfy the public desire for novelty.

James Gurney continued to work in the same hands-on way that he always had with Shaw, supervising the park until 1920. He remained faithful to Shaw's preference for specimen trees and shrubs, and for groupings of related varieties, but his additions were an increasingly abundant and eclectic mix that resulted in highly decorative effects. Plant inventories indicate an impressive collection of hundreds of agaves, palms, bananas, and tree ferns that were displayed in pots. Gurney also added several decorative ponds (installed by special appropriation at his request), and by 1894 he had introduced water lilies at the park; his experiments

Lily pond at Tower Grove Park, ca. 1907.
State Historical Society of Missouri, Columbia.

Tower Grove Park, St. Louis, U. S. A.

Lush plantings at the park, ca. 1907.

in developing seedling nymphaeas produced a unique tricolored striped variety in 1904.[7] The growing of *Victoria* water lilies "as at Regent's Park"[8] would become a Tower Grove Park mainstay, and as a model aquatic garden, it shared information on the growth and habit of the lilies with other institutions.

This different aesthetic sensibility is apparent in annual park reports from 1896 to 1915, and can be attributed not only to Gurney's interest in water lilies but also to changing public taste. The 1899 report indicates that people increasingly anticipated the decorative effects of vivid tints and bright designs; it suggests that adding ornamentation of the park was a priority, the board sanctioning the introduction of parterres and combined floral effects as elements of interest and beauty.[9] Shaw's original emphasis on specimen plantings, for viewing in the round as if they were sculpture, was modified by extravagant mass plantings, particularly around the lily ponds and entrances. Adding flower beds reflected a trend that had begun in London parks, prompted by the belief that floral displays not only supplied a "feast of color" that appealed to the masses but that flowers, too, could be effective tools in the goal of cultivating the undereducated.[10] After the turn of the twentieth century, subsequent maturing of trees and specimen plantings, and Missouri's hot, humid summers, resulted in a luxurious, almost exotic atmosphere, one that was recorded on postcards and in photographs well into the century.

The *Victorias* grown by Gurney at Tower Grove Park loved the longer, hotter Missouri summers, so that they flourished and flowered when grown outside. (In England, they would flower only inside greenhouses.) Their white flowers bloomed at night (they were fully open at midnight) and closed in the morning, and turned pink with age. The appearance and fragrance of these exotic beauties, which attracted sphinx moths, drew crowds of visitors to the heated pools, and special facilities and lighting were set up to allow viewers to enjoy the evening display.[11] Their scent was heavy with the fragrance of tuberose, pineapple, and banana, their seed pods were the size of baseballs, and their giant round leaves with upturned edges were supported beneath by a rigid geomet-

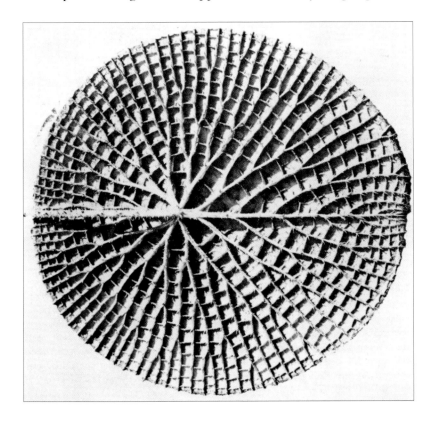

Underside of a Victoria water lily.
From Missouri Botanical Garden Bulletin, *November 1963 (photo by Paul A. Kohl).*

James Gurney standing on a Victoria lily pad.

ric network of ribs. Individual *Victoria* leaves grew up to eight feet in diameter and could support up to 150 pounds if boards were put under the leaves to help distribute the weight, and it became fashionable to have one's picture taken standing or seated on these "water platters."

After 1900, the expense of labor-intensive maintenance and the need for modernization induced the park board to make further changes. The charming hemlock labyrinth and the observatory that anchored its center were removed in 1908 (the observatory was rebuilt using photographs and now stands at the edge of a new maze in the Botanical Garden); the east gatehouse and Tunica's north gate police office were removed in 1912–13, and all wells were closed for health reasons three years later. These losses were balanced by improvements that included the widening of drives, the installation of comfort stations and electric lights throughout the park, and the addition of areas for more active sports—ballfields, tennis courts, and a wading pool.

In comparison with those at the park, the changes in the garden after 1889 were dramatic, sweeping away the old for the new. As a template on which to base future changes, a plan of the garden as it existed in 1889, indicating precise placement of plants, walks, and structures, was drawn and published as a five-page document in the first annual report. The initial work after Shaw's death addressed maintenance of infrastructure and removal or rearrangement of secondary elements within the overall plan. For example, a small labyrinth at the southern end of the arboretum was removed in 1892, replaced by a rockery of Ozark stone and a Mexican garden of succulents and cacti. Two years later the

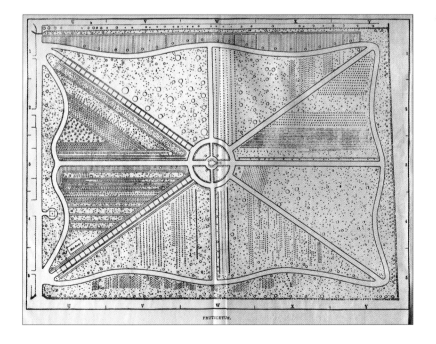

Here and on the following pages, the five-part plan of the garden in 1889.

Fruticetum.

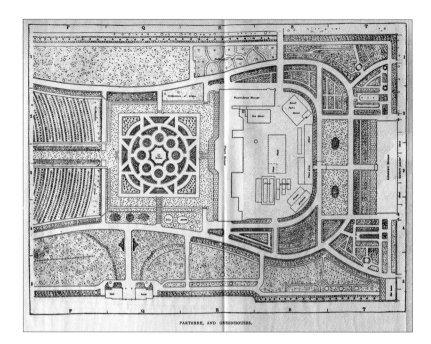

PARTERRE, AND GREENHOUSES.

Sunken parterre and greenhouse.

GROVE, AND HERBACEOUS GROUNDS.

Herbaceous grounds and grove.

"Beauty, Instructiveness & Adaptability to Research"

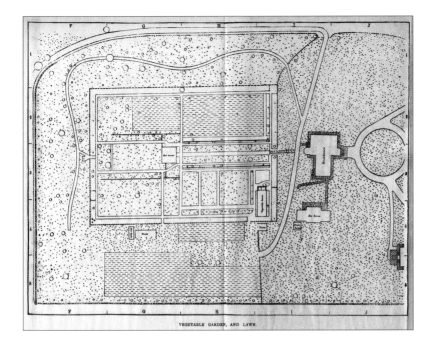

VEGETABLE GARDEN, AND LAWN.

Vegetable garden and lawn.

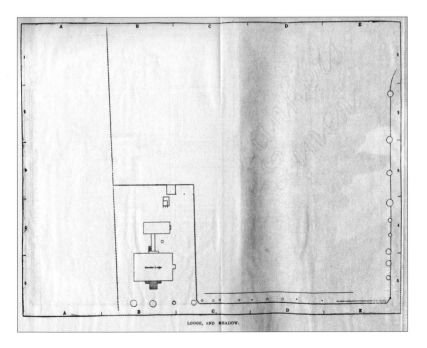

LODGE, AND MEADOW.

Lodge and meadow.

grounds around the observation pavilion in the central parterre were covered in turf, the walks were broadened, and the plants rearranged into natural-looking groups, in contrast with the ringed beds in botanical sequence that had provided order previously. A wild garden, and new plantings, especially near the main entrance, provided additional color. Several "granitoid" ponds for water lilies, one of them in a sinuous shape evoking the slow-moving rivers of South America, were installed in 1894. Newspaper accounts of these "Amazon lilies" increased attendance by one-third, up to 30,151 visitors one Sunday afternoon in September 1896. Along the principal walks radiating from the center of the fruticetum (now more frequently called the orchard) hedges of low-growing fruit-bearing shrubs were added in 1896, as were plants of Japanese origin, contributed by Charles Sprague Sargent of Harvard's Arnold Arboretum.[12]

As designated in Shaw's will, and as a response to the continued need for trained gardeners in the United States, the garden began to recruit intelligent, energetic students from beyond the local area. Announcements in journals such as the English publication *The Gardeners' Chronicle* were directed to young men between the ages of fourteen and twenty.[13] The establishment of scholarships, made possible by funding stipulated in Shaw's will, provided the training of "practical gardeners" who wished to learn garden botany firsthand. Upon acceptance, each student would be taken on for a period of six years, working and receiving practical and theoretical instruction in horticulture, economic entomology, surveying, and bookkeeping "as is necessary for a gardener having the charge of a large estate." Over the six-year period the student's duties included working from five to ten hours per day, depending on the season, and time spent in instruction; reading journal articles related to flower and vegetable gardening and small fruit and orchid culture; taking courses in forestry, surveying, landscape gardening, ferns, and "trees in their winter condition"; and learning the theoretical aspects of their particular interest.[14] Such instruction, which would con-

The Casino.

Photo by Boehl & Koenig.

tinue at the garden until the 1930s, was meant to make gardeners, rather than botanists, and a taste for manual labor was an im-
perative. For their work the students received wages, instruction
at the School of Botany at Washington University, and plain and
comfortable lodgings. Early on, students stayed in a structure at
the southern end of the Shaw estate, facing the park, which
served alternately as worker housing, a teahouse, and a restaurant
called "The Casino," a reference to its function as a place in the
country or garden used for entertainment.[15]

In 1895 a long-range plan for development of the garden was
requested by the trustees. There were immediate practical needs
to be dealt with such as renovation of the power plant,[16] and the
financial strain caused by the tax burden of unused land west of
Grand Avenue.[17] Director Trelease presented the board with a
summary of accomplishments and a plan, which he had been at
work on for two years, that proposed new acreage for development, new conservatories, and new research facilities. He

View of the North American tract showing farm buildings, Tower Grove House, the museum building, and the mausoleum, 1900.

North American tract, south end of the larger lake, 1907.

"Beauty, Instructiveness & Adaptability to Research"

outlined specific plantings, educational needs, and research priorities and presented an organized sequence of development.[18] An
additional 82.5 acres of contiguous Shaw property that was being
used as pasture and farmland would be earmarked for future extension of the garden.[19] Of that parcel, twenty acres were to be
planted as a collection of flora of the United States, and the remaining sixty-two acres represented flora of the world, the two
merging, according to Trelease, into a "single piece of artistic
landscape." Each would be "synoptically arranged" according to
the natural affinities of plants as outlined by the botanists George
Bentham and Joseph Hooker in their *Genera Plantarum* for the
smaller tract[20] and by Adolph Engler and Karl Prantl in *Die
Pflanzenfamilien*, for the larger tract.

Most, but not all, of the trustees were convinced of the plan's
balance of interests for the public and the scientific commu-

*Planting of cattails in
the North American
tract, 1903.*

nity—or, as Trelease referred to them, the casual visitor and the careful student. In spite of the mandate of public education, the board may have feared the scientific organization of the new parcel too pedantic for a broad audience, even if the visitor were provided with Gray's *Manual of Botany* as a guide, as later *Garden Bulletins* suggested. In Trelease's attention to research and extension of the library and herbarium holdings (and related staff) some of the board members sensed an interest in "more science and less garden."[21]

Trelease believed that the garden proper—Shaw's sunken parterre and herbaceous grounds—fell far short of what it could be. The director's "radical and wholesale renovation" would remove the colorful and profuse arrangement; those who embraced decorative gardening understood that his plan would change the very nature of the garden Shaw had made.[22] An even greater concern was his proposed location for a new conservatory, placed so it could be seen from Tower Grove and Magnolia Avenues, which would threaten Shaw's museum and villa. The idea of tearing down Shaw's house to "make room for buildings of modern character," as reported in the *St. Louis Post-Dispatch*, galvanized public sentiment. Certain members of the board, who believed that the proposal went against the mandates of Shaw's will, objected.[23] The director called promotion of his plan "hard and uphill."[24]

The board did agree that extension of the garden was an important first step, and in January 1896 Trelease submitted the plan he had been at work on for over two years to the firm of Olmsted, Olmsted and Eliot, of Brookline, Massachusetts.[25] Within a week the firm responded, and in April "Mr. Olmsted" arrived in St. Louis for a board meeting to discuss Trelease's plan, which was approved with the exception of a few minor details.[26] Those reluctant to change the garden would seem to have had little choice. The Olmsted firm was respected and well known, and consultation with them certainly worked in Trelease's favor. But ultimately the impetus for going forward was provided by nature, not prestige or consensus. A tornado, which was preceded by a devastating hailstorm, ripped through the neighborhood on May 27, 1896, severely damaging four hundred fifty trees and thousands of panes of conservatory glass at the garden alone. Addressing the results of this destruction, Trelease called for the "clearing, to a very large extent, and suitable rearranging and replanting of the entire tract."[27]

For nearly ten years the Missouri Botanical Garden and the Olmsted firm worked to agree on a plan.[28] A contract was signed on August 10, 1896, and in December of that year the firm recorded sixteen pages describing the strengths and weaknesses of the existing garden, with suggestions for future plans. These observations were the basis of the nineteen-page *Formal Report Accompanying Preliminary Plans* submitted by Olmsted Sr. and his stepson and partner John Charles Olmsted in June 1897. This re-

Tornado damage in the Botanical Garden, May 27, 1896.

port acknowledged the importance of history to the garden, stating that Shaw's improvements should be preserved and embodied in future plans, partly because of the influence of nostalgia on public sentiment.[29] Several recommendations differed from Trelease's plan: the Olmsted firm suggested tearing down the museum building ("built of cheap materials . . . already crumbling to pieces"), aligning the main gate with Flora Avenue on the east side, and changing the decorative sunken parterre to serve a "useful purpose for special collections." They disagreed with Trelease's first choice of location for the new palm house (south of Shaw's villa) and suggested it be placed to the west of the existing one. During this period preliminary issues of grading, drainage, and the recording of topography were addressed. Detailed plans were drawn and plant lists were formulated for the collections of North American and world (or "universal") flora, which included ten pages of plantings—eighteen large beds, the "singular" planting of trees, an abundant use of vines such as trumpet creeper (*Campsis radicans*) and, in one section, 525 Virginia creeper, now *Parthenocissus quinquefolia* (which Downing had praised earlier in the century, saying it shined like "foliage on fire").

During these years of planning, Trelease communicated about gardens and plants with horticulturists and landscape architects about gardens and plants, including Thomas Meehan, Harvard's John Allen, Charles Sprague Sargent of the Arnold Arboretum, Liberty Hyde Bailey of Cornell, and the landscape architect Warren Manning of Boston. In 1898, he went to England and Europe to visit botanical gardens and herbaria, including, on the suggestion of John Charles Olmsted, historic parks and gardens. Olmsted told Trelease that he should be certain to see Edouard François André's public gardens on the Riviera at Monte Carlo, and the work of William Robinson and Robert Marnock near London, which he considered to be the "most nearly successful example of the almost hopeless attempt to imitate Nature in city parks."[30] Olmsted admired Robinson, editor of *The Garden*, for his use of native plants and his hatred of the popular Victorian method of planting called carpet bedding (Robinson boasted that he was a "flower gardener, not a spreader of bad carpets"). But it is interesting that Olmsted should recommend Marnock, whose work included the gardenesque method at the Sheffield Botanic Garden, an approach he abhorred.[31] It was the shared appreciation for more natural effects that had drawn Trelease to the Olmsted firm, and he agreed with Olmsted Sr. that the mania for "brilliant and gaudy decoration under the name of specimen gardening, bedding, carpet, embroidery, & ribbon gardening" sacrificed the beauty of natural scenery.[32]

Trelease hoped to rid the Missouri Botanical Garden of precisely these methods, and the intricate, labor-intensive parterres and vine-embellished gazebos of Shaw's era. The garden seemed old-fashioned and crowded; an editing of the profuse visual effect, created by the multitude of plants elaborately arranged and decorated with paths, urns, and gazebos, was needed. The May tornado offered the opportunity, and the Trelease plan, supported by the Olmsted firm's recommendations, provided the means not only to replace and repair but to begin anew in terms of taste.

The final plan submitted by the firm, dated 1905, sympathetically combined the key historic and the new elements.[33] In addition to the proposed grounds devoted to North American and world flora, they recommended a series of French, English, Italian, and Dutch formal parterres to be aligned along the eastern periphery.[34] The herbaceous grounds and observatory (renamed the Pagoda Garden) and Shaw's villa and museum block to the southeast were to be retained. The central glass conservatory Shaw had built thirty-six years earlier would be eliminated to clear the way for a new primary (east-west) axis, anchored at one end by a monumental conservatory with terrace gardens and by the improved Flora Avenue gate at the other.[35] The Olmsted firm suggested that this new conservatory, "a great museum of living plants," have a curving roof of considerable height and be built on a nave-and-transept plan similar to Christian churches. The inte-

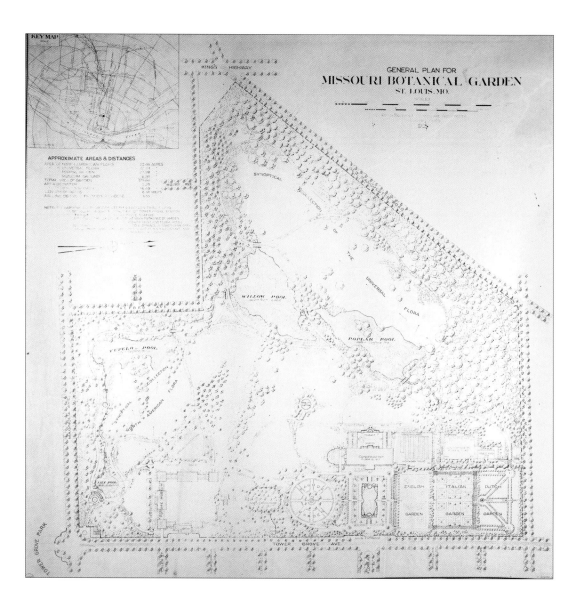

The Olmsted final plan, 1905.

rior organization would be similar to the conservatory at Syon House (across the Thames from Kew), or the one at the Frankfurt botanical garden, both known for their effective displays. The proposed acreage of American and world flora would extend to Kingshighway, utilizing much of the unimproved Shaw property to the west.

Between 1897 and 1904 a series of different plans and suggestions were submitted by the Olmsted firm,[36] but by 1900 a lack of consensus about the project and a sense of uneasiness about progress had become evident. Holding on to their memory of Henry Shaw and to the directives of his will, critics challenged the replacement of the original garden; tensions between the trustees and Trelease came to a head. Newspaper articles reported on the debate, and an argumentative tone could be discerned in correspondence from the new president of the board (who referred to Trelease as the "new ruler"). In December 1904 the board voted to terminate the agreement with the Olmsted firm, believing that "the matter should be closed up and further expense in the direction stopped."[37] Upon receipt of the Olmsteds' detailed plans, the agreement entered into in 1896 between the trustees and the landscape architects was considered "definitely terminated." Trelease's final letter one month later thanked the firm for their painstaking care and the "worthy ideal" their plan represented, and regretted that the "radical changes to the present flower-garden" and fruticetum they had proposed would not be possible until the future. The lack of unanimous agreement on the garden's improvement and mission which had resulted in a power struggle between the director and the board ended with Trelease's resignation in 1912. Unwilling to compromise his principles of "more garden but no less science," Trelease left and returned to research.

George Moore, a botanist who had joined the garden in 1909 to oversee the graduate program there and at Washington University, took over as director. Working with him was George H. Pring, an orchidologist, born in Exmouth, Devonshire, who had come to the garden in 1906 (after being awarded a Kew scholarship),[38] and a new group of instructors and staff who made aesthetic and scientific contributions. Among this group was landscape architect John Noyes, schooled at the Massachusetts State Agriculture College, who came from the office of Warren Manning in 1913. An increasing number of women students began to attend and graduate from the institution,[39] including Eda Sutermeister, who studied landscape gardening and went on to

work in the firm of George Kessler, the midwestern landscape architect responsible for the Kansas City parks and boulevard system.

The board and garden staff spent the year and a half following Trelease's resignation reviewing proposed changes. Their 1914 plan, which includes suggestions by John Noyes, combines many of the ideas Trelease had proposed twenty-four years before and

several of the improvements outlined in the Olmsted master plan. Shaw's monumental conservatory (which included the first plant houses from 1859) was torn down after forty-eight years of use and was replaced by a new palm house sited according to the Olmsted firm's suggestions. Major collections including desert, cycad, economic, and the South African plants, previously exhibited in Shaw's interconnected display houses, were consolidated in the wings of the new palm house (the day it opened, November 16, 1913, ten thousand people visited in three hours). The contents of an existing fern dome were relocated there, too, and a mossy grotto with a stream was added. Juno moved again, from her spot anchoring Shaw's elaborate sunken parterre to a new position in the Italian terrace garden. Foundations, plants, and root systems were excavated, and the ground was graded and reworked. A large water garden surrounded by formal beds

School of Gardening students and instructors, graduation, June 1917. (George Moore at top, George H. Pring back row at left, John Noyes in front of him.)

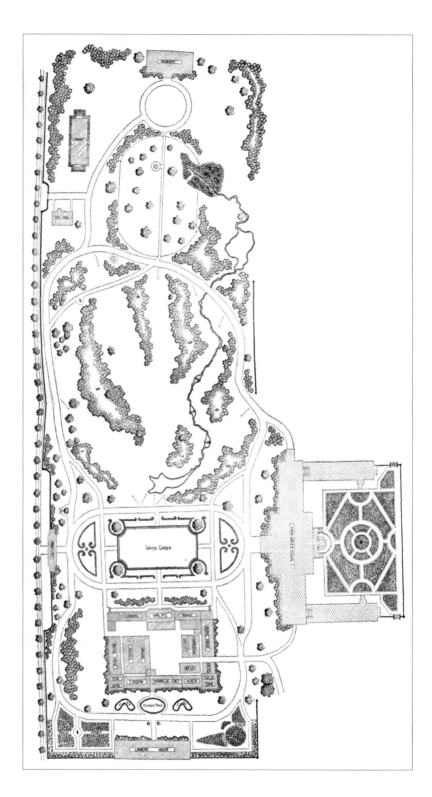

Plan for the Missouri Botanical Garden, with contributions by John Noyes, ca. 1917.

OPPOSITE:
Palm House, October 1914.

Planting palms in the Palm House, 1913.

Fern House,
pre-1920.

Plants removed from
the herbaceous
grounds in
preparation for
renovation.

(slightly French in character) and a wooded area called "the Knolls" replaced Shaw's structured botanical sequence.[40]

Garden Bulletin articles documenting these changes helped the public envision the garden before and after. Director Moore addressed the theoretical aspects of the changes by outlining the principles that guide the landscape gardener (he equated these with the artistic vision of a landscape painter rather than that of the botanist, as Shaw would have done). He then described the actual improvements, including 3,500 feet of new walks that enabled convenient viewing of new educational and vegetable gardens, plant displays for edging and window boxes, grasses, and hardy climbers. A hundred-square-foot grandmother's garden was planted in the "reckless profusion" characteristic of old-fashioned gardens.[41] The naturalistic yet constructed series of hills and valleys of the Knolls included native plants—willows near ponds and the stream, for example—but it also showcased a sur-

Juno and garden employees in the Italian garden.

prising choice and arrangement of plantings that Shaw himself could have chosen. One knoll was covered with elephant ears backed by pokeweed (*Phytolacca*); one displayed the garden's fine collection of cannas; another was covered with a shrubby mix of hydrangeas, forsythia, and mock orange—and each knoll was ringed with flower borders.[42] Two new horseshoe-shaped water gardens, which flanked the Victoria Pond, displayed a mix of water lilies such as the huge *Victoria cruziana*, the dark red and deep blue day-blooming lilies whose colors were perfected by James Gurney (and descendants of the first lilies propagated at Tower Grove Park). Many of the huge number of plants removed from the former parterres were reused. Four large American hollies

Lily ponds and the main gardens, 1918.

Pond of hardy lilies west of the pergola, 1922.

taken from the observatory were repositioned at the corners of the Victoria Pond, and thirty large trees were transplanted for immediate effect the following spring.

What changed most dramatically between 1913 and 1917, however, was the nucleus of the original garden. Using the very style that Shaw had steadfastly chosen not to employ, garden officials—responding to contemporary taste and an interest in

The Knolls, looking southeast, 1923.

progress—remade the sunken parterre and the herbaceous grounds into a pastoral sweep of parklike space.

In May 1913, the *Garden Bulletin* proudly explained that "nothing of the old arrangement remains to indicate where things formerly were. In place of the flat, hedge-covered plain, with its myriads of small beds and maze of walks, there is now a rolling landscape, covered with shrubbery and flowers, with long stretches of lawn broken by a small stream and its accompanying pools."[43] Shaw's original aesthetic had been replaced with the effect of a naturalistic landscape that, according to contemporary taste, was "more pleasing and restful than any formal garden could ever be."

Afterword

This study by Carol Grove significantly advances our understanding of the background of Tower Grove Park and the Missouri Botanical Garden. Her research has marshaled known sources and also made some new connections that help to illuminate this period in the history of American landscape design through the prism of one visionary philanthropist's experiences.

Henry Shaw's vision can fairly be characterized as personalized, even in some respects idiosyncratic, but the efficacy of his efforts, their durability and flexibility, remain in place for all to see and admire. Both of his offspring institutions have made, and continue to make, substantial contributions to the community of which they are an integral part, and in the case of the Garden, also to the broader world of international science and conservation.

Following Shaw's lifetime, both the Garden and the Park at one time or another, to one degree or another, have experienced difficulties with funding and maintenance. The growth and development of the Garden under the leadership of Dr. Peter Raven since 1971 is a tale of legendary proportions, and worthy of some future book of its own.

The story of the Park since Shaw is less dramatic but also of

*Morning view in
the park.*
Photo by Carol Betsch.

great interest, and salutary in a number of important ways. As for so many public open spaces in urban America, the mid-twentieth century was a low point for Tower Grove Park. People seemed to be turning their backs on the centers of big cities all across our land, and in the process all but abandoning the urban parks in those cities. Tower Grove was no exception to this trend, and the effects of deferred maintenance, inadequate funding, and general decline took their toll and augured ominously for the future.

Tower Grove Park, however, harbored key underlying assets, even in the darkest of times: a dedicated and politically independent board of commissioners, a fervent if then small and unorganized constituency, and a design of magical inherent appeal, which included an ensemble of original structures and features of extraordinary charm and historical significance, essentially unaltered even if they were worn and tired. The integrity of Shaw's nineteenth-century design was almost miraculously intact.

A crusade of sorts was undertaken from the late 1980s which mobilized the latent energies of the various Park constituencies, including the commissioners, the staff, the surrounding neighborhoods, hundreds of volunteers and donors, and a new organization regional in scope, the Friends of Tower Grove Park. Models of park renewal campaigns from around the nation, such as at New York's Central Park, and from our own region, such as at Forest Park, were also studied and consulted.

The various Tower Grove groups have worked together to bring about a major renaissance of the Park as a specimen of nineteenth-century park landscape design unparalleled in its comprehensive authenticity. Not coincidentally, this renaissance also renewed the Park as a living force for urban vitality and civility in the most diverse and densely built up portion of one of America's older and prouder cities. This renaissance has had an exhilarating effect on all of those involved, and proven a wonderful benefit for the quality of life in the city of St. Louis.

A key milestone in this renewal was the Park's designation in 1989 as a National Historic Landmark; at that time it was only the fourth urban park to be so honored. This landmark status, besides helping to draw philanthropic support, has also helped to ensure that the sometimes hectic pace of various restorations and renovations has been tempered and guided by the spirit and principles of the rapidly emerging science and art of historic landscape conservation.

Dilapidated structures perforce have been addressed as a priority. More attention as well is now being focused on the living landscape. As was pointed out in the foreword to this book, the Park in recent times has come to convey a bit more of a picturesque impression than its original gardenesque conception. In part, this is owing to several twentieth-century decades of inadequate funding, during which it was not possible to replace choice flowering and specimen trees, the few plantings done were of the least expensive and most conveniently accessible types, and actual installations reflected a certain aesthetic "drift" away from the clarity of Shaw's design. Partly also, the inadequacy of funding for proper pruning and general care has tended to render young and old trees alike less healthy and distinct in appearance.

A new planting plan is now in place, however, based on improved arboriculture and long-term restoration of original landscape values, which are well documented. Comprising a broad but carefully selected palette of woody plant varieties, replacement plantings are gently and gradually restoring much of the original gardenesque aesthetic appeal. The Park thus remains a source not only of urban sylvan beauty but also of great instructional value.

Through all of these efforts, the inherent reasonableness and flexibility of Shaw's plan have been revealed afresh. We and all of our now more than one million annual visitors, in our respective and individual ways, continue to be enriched by that wisdom.

Tower Grove Park and the Missouri Botanical Garden both function very successfully, the Park on a community and regional stage, the Garden on that and also a world stage. And both do so in essentially the manner envisioned by their common founder, Henry Shaw. That is a remarkable testament by any standard, and a legacy of which any philanthropist, any designer, any landscape visionary could be proud indeed.

John Karel
Director
Tower Grove Park

Late afternoon,
Tower Grove Park.

Photo by Carol Betsch.

Notes

Introduction

1. Henry Shaw, "A Guide to the Missouri Botanical Garden," Henry Shaw Papers, box 128, Missouri Botanical Garden (MBG) Archives, St. Louis. Published in *Missouri Botanical Garden Bulletin* (*MBGB*) 31, no. 7 (1943): 135–45, as "Henry Shaw's Idea of a Botanical Garden."
2. "Henry Shaw," *Gardeners' Chronicle,* January 11, 1890, 46.
3. David MacAdam, *Tower Grove Park* (St. Louis: R. P. Studley, 1883), 10–11.
4. Thomas Dimmock, "Henry Shaw, A Biographical Sketch," *Report of the Missouri Botanical Garden* 1 (1889), 16.
5. Loudon was Scottish by birth but practiced and lived in England most of his life. Deborah Cavendish, Duchess of Devonshire, as cited in *The Garden at Chatsworth*
6. (New York: Viking Studio, 1999), 38.
7. Elizabeth Keeney, *The Botanizers: Amateur Scientists in Nineteenth-Century America* (Chapel Hill: University of North Carolina Press, 1992).
8. Ibid., 39.
9. "Henry Shaw," *Gardeners' Chronicle,* 46.

Chapter 1

1. Thomas Dimmock, "Henry Shaw," 8. Dimmock's nineteen-page article, drawn upon liberally here, is the basis for the entry on Shaw in the *Encyclopedia of the History of St. Louis,* vol. 4 (1899), 2051. Dimmock wrote for local newspapers, and he and Shaw were good friends.
2. "Henry Shaw's Alma Mater and Peter Collinson," *MBGB* 19, no. 5 (1931). See

Norman G. Brett-James, *The History of Mill Hill School, 1807–1907* (London: Andrew Melrose, 1911), and Brett-James, *The Life of Peter Collinson* (c. 1925). See also William Faherty, *Henry Shaw: His Life and Legacies* (Columbia: University of Missouri Press, 1987), 6–7.

3. "Henry Shaw's Alma Mater," 92. Loudon also mentions the botanical garden at Mill Hill in his *Encyclopedia of Gardening,* 1850 edition.

4. In 1825 Ridgeway House was demolished and replaced by a large classical building designed by William Tite, which is still in use today.

5. See David Philip Miller and Peter Hanns Reill, eds., *Visions of Empire: Voyages, Botany, and Representations of Nature* (Cambridge, U.K.: Cambridge University Press, 1996), 5.

6. Henry Shaw Papers, Inventory of 1889, MBG Archives, cites Shaw's ownership of works by Humboldt and Bonpland. He also owned the work of Michaux and Thomas Nuttall, the English plant collector who traveled in the upper midwestern United States and lower Mississippi Valley.

7. "Reminiscences" of Henry Shaw, in the *Missouri Republican*, May 4, 1869.

8. Little more than a decade before Shaw's arrival conditions were much less settled: Lewis and Clark had just returned from charting the Pacific Northwest, the territory had yet to become a state, and Native Americans were attacking Missouri settlements.

9. For a good general history of the city, see James Neil Primm, *Lion of the Valley: St. Louis, Missouri, 1764–1980*, 3d ed. (St. Louis: Missouri Historical Society, 1998). Lawrence Lowic's *The Architectural Heritage of St. Louis 1803–1891* (St. Louis: Washington University Gallery of Art, 1982) remains the best critique of its nineteenth-century architectural development. Eric Sandweiss, *St. Louis: The Evolution of an American Urban Landscape* (Philadelphia: Temple University Press, 2001), provides an assessment of the city and how it evolved from the early nineteenth century to the present. For views and accounts by artists and authors of the last century, also see two books by John W. Reps, *Saint Louis Illustrated: Nineteenth-Century Engravings and Lithographs of a Mississippi River Metropolis* (Columbia: University of Missouri Press, 1989) and *Cities of the Mississippi: Nineteenth-Century Images of Urban Development* (Columbia: University of Missouri Press, 1994).

10. John A. Paxton's *The St. Louis Directory and Register Containing the Names, Professions, and Residences of all the Heads of Families and Persons in Business . . .* (St. Louis: Printed for the Publisher, 1821) listed many of the business, professional, and industrial activities in the city in 1821, including examples that suggest refined living, such as musicians, a portrait painter, potteries, confectioners, and cordial distilleries. As cited in Reps, *St. Louis Illustrated*, 19.

11. King, *The Great South*, as cited in Reps, *Cities of the Mississippi*, 186.

12. This description comes from Shaw's recollections, documented in his *Guide to the Missouri Botanical Garden*, which he wrote sometime around 1880. Henry Shaw Papers, Box 128, MBG Archives.

13. Caroline Shaw to Henry Shaw, Pittsford, New York, August 8, 1830. MBG Archives.

14. In 1820, the year after Shaw arrived, 1,860 slaves constituted the basis of the labor force in St. Louis County. Shaw owned eleven slaves until 1853, many of whom were replaced by Bohemian immigrants. See Antonio F. Holland, "African Americans in Henry Shaw's St. Louis," 56, in Sandweiss, ed., *St. Louis in the Century of Henry Shaw: A View Beyond the Garden Wall* (Columbia: University of Missouri Press, 2003).

15. Dimmock, "Henry Shaw," 11. In today's economy the amount would be approximately $380,000.00. At his death, Shaw was worth over two million dollars.

16. The acreage where Shaw's villa would be built was purchased at a sheriff's sale on August 27, 1842, for $95.00.

17. The book, *On Laying Out, Planting, and Managing of Cemeteries and on the Improvement of Churchyards* (1843, reprint ed. by James Steves Curl. Redhills, Surrey, U.K.: Ivelet Books, 1981), is inscribed on the inside "From the Author, April 27, 1843" in Shaw's handwriting.

18. Shaw owned Gilpin's *Observations on the River Wye* (1782) and the *Lake District* (1789), tour books that educated the viewer on the picturesque landscape. He also owned Edmund Burke's *An Enquiry into the Sublime and the Beautiful* (1757), an essay on the aesthetics of, and human response to, the sublime and the beautiful in objects and in nature.

19. The merging of "colonial memories, capitalist opportunity, and republican ideals" that shaped the character of St. Louis and created its prosperity would peak by 1850, but the population would continue to increase, to over 160,700 in the following decade, to exceed that of Chicago. See Sandweiss, *St. Louis*, 37.

20. Shaw owned lots at the corner of First and Market, Fourth and Locust, Sixth and Market, and Seventh and Pine, and whole blocks such as that defined by Sixth, St. Charles, Seventh, and Washington Streets.

21. Francis Grierson, *The Valley of Shadows* (London: Bradbury Agnew, 1909), 215, as cited in Faherty, *Henry Shaw,* 58.

22. Ibid.

23. Charles van Ravenswaay, *Saint Louis: An Informal History of the City and Its People, 1764–1865* (St. Louis: Missouri Historical Society Press, 1991), 237.

24. Originally part of the city commons and reserved as a parade ground, Lafayette Park was designated for park purposes in 1851. In 1864 it would be landscaped by the noteworthy Maximillian G. Kern, designer of Forest Park and the grounds of many of the prestigious homes that flanked it at Westmoreland and Portland Places.

25. The adjacent property was planned as the site for a reservoir to supply water for Tower Grove, and ultimately, in 1899, the Compton Water Tower was built there. See Carolyn Hewes Toft, *St. Louis: Landmarks & Historic Districts* (St. Louis: Landmarks Association of St. Louis, Inc., 2002).

26. Plant names and botanical nomenclature are presented here as Shaw recorded

them, indicating his use of both botanical Latin and common names for plants as he saw fit.

27. First identified in 1804 by Meriwether Lewis and William Clark in 1804 (who sent slips to Thomas Jefferson from the St. Louis garden of Pierre Chouteau), the Osage orange tree was known for its strength and flexibility. In *Rural Essays* (1853), A. J. Downing praised the tree and suggested it was destined to become a favorite in all the southern and western portions of the country. It became extremely popular in the nineteenth century for its practical application as impenetrable fencing.

28. Wilhelm Miller, *The Prairie Spirit in Landscape Gardening* (1915) (Amherst: University of Massachusetts Press and the Library of American Landscape History, 2002), 29.

29. Ibid., xx.

30. J. E. Spingarn, "HWS and the English Landscape Tradition at Wodenethe: An English Inheritance Becomes an American Influence," *Landscape Architecture* 29 (1939): 37.

31. Brent Elliott, *Victorian Gardens* (Portland, Ore.: Timber Press, 1986), 123–28. The principles of color theory were put into practice by John Caie, head gardener for the duke of Bedford at Bedford Lodge, Kensington. Color theory was an important topic in horticultural journals such as the *Cottage Gardener,* botanist John Lindley commented on the theory of Michel-Eugène Chevreul, and Charles Eastlake translated Goethe's *Theory of Colors* in 1840.

32. Alfred George Stevens (1817–75), a respected Victorian artist, sculptor, and teacher, was one of only six English sculptors honored by representation on the facade of the Victoria & Albert Museum—the British National Museum of Art and Design—where several of his works are now part of the permanent collection. His fire surround exhibited at the 1851 Great Exhibition is part of the collection, as are a fire surround made at the Coalbrookdale factory (exhibited at the 1862 London Exhibition), a small iron and marble table (1868) designed for the Refreshment Room at the Victoria & Albert, and cast-iron lions made for the British Museum railings. He worked as chief designer for Henry E. Hoole's manufacturing company during his most creative period, from 1850 to 1857.

Chapter 2

1. He also mentioned his plan to give the city a tract of land for a public park. Richard Smith Elliott, *Notes Taken in Sixty Years* (St. Louis: R. F. Studley, 1883), 279, as cited in Faherty, *Henry Shaw.* Faherty was the first to look at Shaw in depth and in the context of the nineteenth century.

2. A lesser-known 1835 work by the landscape gardener Jonas Dennis was also in Shaw's collection, inscribed on the title page "To Joseph Paxton Esq." How it came into Shaw's collection is unknown, but Shaw and Paxton could have met

in Matlock on Shaw's first return trip in 1840. Paxton was a landowner in Matlock, and his wife's family was from there; at the time Paxton was building cottages in the area as well as writing for horticultural journals and working at Chatsworth.

3. Shaw did not list journals in the 1854 inventory of his country house, but they were listed in a later inventory of his town house. Those included A. J. Downing's *The Horticulturalist,* John Claudius Loudon's *Gardener's Magazine* (1826–43), and Lindley and Paxton's *Gardeners' Chronicle* (from 1841), considered by many to be the finest of the genre.

4. Henry Shaw to George Engelmann, October 18, 1856, George Engelmann Letters, MBG Archives (hereafter cited as GEL). Shaw also told Engelmann, "All this I am doing according to my ideas gathered from horticultural works of Loudon, McIntosh etc. . . no one here can give me the least information—." Shaw to Engelmann, September 15, 1857, GEL.

5. See Deborah Cavendish, Duchess of Devonshire, *The Garden at Chatsworth* (New York: Viking Studio, 1999), and Candice A. Shoemaker, ed., "Chatsworth Gardens," in *Encyclopedia of Gardens: History and Design* (Chicago: Fitzroy Dearborn, 2001).

6. In England the visiting of houses and grounds had become a pastime for proper society in the eighteenth century. Thomas Jefferson and John Adams, for example, toured English ornamental farms and gardens in 1786, including Stowe, a mandatory stop on the circuit with its follies and landscape park. The practice was so routine that it became subject matter in novels: in *Pride and Prejudice* Jane Austen's Elizabeth Bennet took the fashionable picturesque tour of Derbyshire, visiting the fictitious Pemberley (possibly based on Chatsworth).

7. *Derbyshire Courier, Chesterfield Gazette and General County Advertiser,* June 30, 1849, as cited in Cavendish, *The Garden at Chatsworth,* 84.

8. Shaw to William Jackson Hooker, February 11, 1856.

9. John Claudius Loudon toured the Sheffield garden in 1839 and published an account of it that same year.

10. Marnock was a contemporary of Shaw—their dates, 1800–1889, correspond exactly—and it is possible they met again later at the Regent's Park gardens of the Royal Botanic Society, where Marnock served as curator, after he left Sheffield, until 1869. James Gurney, the man who would become Shaw's gardener in 1867, was employed at Regent's Park before he left for America in 1866.

11. The pay scale was based on qualifications: laborers received 87 cents, bricklayers $1.75, and the superintendent, George Pipe, was paid $2.00 per half day.

12. See Patricia Timberlake, "George Engelmann, 1809–1884: Early Missouri Botanist," *Missouri Folklore Society Journal* 10 (1988): 1–8. See also Patricia Timberlake, "George Engelmann: Scientist at the Gateway to the American West, 1809–1860," master's thesis, University of Missouri–Columbia, 1984.

The term "Midwest" postdates Shaw's and Engelmann's arrival (Shaw specifically located St. Louis in the Mississippi Valley), yet the concept is born of, and coincides with, the nineteenth-century westward expansion which they were a part of and the country that was created as a result. Both individuals appreciated St. Louis, Missouri's location as the gateway to the West, the midpoint between the East Coast and the western territories. Today the term is defined as a region of northern states from Ohio west to the Rocky Mountains. Missouri is on the southern edge of this range of states and alternately can be considered northern or southern depending on views that date to the sectional division of the Civil War. Recent research in the field of landscape history has worked to illustrate the sense of place unique to each of these regions, interpreting the differences between the landscapes of, for example, the East and the Midwest. (See William H. Tishler, ed., *Midwestern Landscape Architecture* [Urbana: University of Illinois Press/Library of American Landscape History, 2000].)

13. The French had settled the city, and in 1850, 43 percent of the population were immigrants, many German natives. Primm, *Lion of the Valley,* 172–73.

14. The publication so impressed the writer Goethe that he offered Engelmann his own botanical notes and sketches.

15. A. Hunter Dupree, *Asa Gray, 1810–1888* (New York: Atheneum, 1968), 157–58, and Timberlake, *Engelmann: Scientist*, 53.

16. Richard Beidelman, "George Engelmann: Botanical Gatekeeper of the West," *Horticulture* 48 (April 1970): 4, 42.

17. See Dupree, *Asa Gray*, 159–67, for a discussion of Engelmann and these plant collectors. Also see George Yatskievych, *Steyermark's Flora of Missouri*, vol. 1, rev. ed. (Jefferson City: Missouri Dept. of Conservation in cooperation with the Missouri Botanical Garden, 1999), 12–16, and Asa Gray to George Engelmann, May 30, 1846, as cited in Jane Loring Gray, ed., *The Letters of Asa Gray,* vol. 1 (Boston: Houghton Mifflin, 1973), 341.

18. Michael Long, "George Engelmann and the Lure of Frontier Science," *Missouri Historical Review* 89, no. 3 (April 1995): 252. "Engelmann observed and collected in Humboldtian fashion to increase his total understanding of the western frontier" (260).

19. Yatskievych, *Steyermark's Flora*, 14.

20. Joseph Ewan, ed., *A Short History of Botany in the United States* (New York: Hafner Pub. Co., 1969), 43.

21. Primm, *Lion of the Valley,* 196.

22. Scientific papers were published in its journal, *Transactions,* beginning in 1857. The Academy, the first of its kind west of the Allegheny Mountains, facilitated study and promoted communication between scientists in St. Louis and around the world. See Timberlake, *Engelmann: Scientist*, 98–104.

23. Yatskievych, *Steyermark's Flora*, 14.

24. Engelmann's herbarium became the core of the Missouri Botanical Garden collection. Letters to Asa Gray indicate that Engelmann had planned to contribute his herbarium to the Missouri collection after his death. In their correspondence is discussion of purchase and shipment of paper type and size chosen to coincide

with that being used at the garden herbarium, the aim being to ease the process of adding specimens to the existing collection while ensuring consistency.

25. Engelmann's collected works were published posthumously in 1887 by editors Asa Gray and William Trelease (who would later become the director of Shaw's Garden). Asa Gray and William Trelease, eds., *The Botanical Works of the Late George Engelmann, Collected for Henry Shaw, Esq.* (Cambridge, Mass.: John Wilson and Son, 1887). A copy of the *Works* was given by Shaw to Joseph D. Hooker at Kew in 1888. Copies were acquired by the Massachusetts Horticultural Society and the Huntington Library, San Marino, California.

26. Born in Sauquoit, Oneida County, New York, Gray received a medical degree from the Fairfield Medical School (New York) in 1831. The definitive work on Asa Gray remains Dupree, *Asa Gray*.

27. Yatskievych, *Steyermark's Flora*, 14.

28. Gray's later publications include his *School and Field Book of Botany* (1857) and *Manual of the Botany of the Northern United States* (1848, with five subsequent editions within his lifetime), which made important contributions to education in this country. His work on the flora of eastern North America and Japan, published in *Memoirs of the American Academy of Arts and Sciences* (1859), remains one of his most important contributions to research.

29. "Asa Gray," *American National Biography*, vol. 9 (New York: Oxford University Press, 1999), 439–40.

30. Asa Gray, "George Engelmann," *American Journal of Science* 28 (July–December 1884): 61–67.

31. Beidelman, "George Engelmann."

32. Engelmann to Gray, July 27, 1843, as cited in Timberlake, *Engelmann: Scientist*, 51.

33. Engelmann to Asa Gray, April 9, 1856, as cited in "Formative Days of Mr. Shaw's Garden," *MBGB* 40, no. 5 (1942): 101.

34. "He [Shaw] has already had a letter from Hooker referring him to me! Which had a good effect." Engelmann to Gray, May 13, 1856, as cited in ibid.

35. See John Claudius Loudon, *Encyclopedia of Gardening* (Book 3: The Practice of Horticulture), 735–41: Loudon notes "the importance of entering the garden from the south, south-east, or south-west sides; and this circumstance must not be lost sight of for main entrances. . . . Doors, in short, should be so contrived, as never to invite visitors to the north slip, or so as to get behind the hothouses [which must always face south]." The orientation of the conservatory to the main display garden is strikingly similar to that illustrated in the encyclopedia.

36. Shaw to Hooker, February 11, 1856. North American Letters, 1851–1858, archives of the Royal Botanic Garden, Kew. Copies exist in the MBG Archives.

37. A variation of this idea was used to generate income for the garden. Shaw Place, which included ten houses that rented for $50 to $55 per month, was built a few blocks east of the garden in 1878–83. See Carolyn Toft, *St. Louis: Landmarks & Historic Districts* (St. Louis: Landmarks Association of St. Louis), 236–37.

38. Shaw to Hooker, December 18, 1857.

39. Shaw to Hooker, August 10, 1856.

40. Hooker to Shaw, August 10, 1857.

41. "If each [garden] is consistent with good taste & in convenience of study, such variety is not only allowable but agreeable." Ibid.

42. Shaw did not see this as a top priority. In responding to Hooker's advice, he said that the purchase of a large number of books would not take place until the building of his museum and library was complete, not before 1860. Shaw to Hooker, December 18, 1857, North American Letters, Kew.

43. Hooker to Shaw, January 27, 1858, MBG Archives.

44. Shaw to Engelmann, January 13, 1858, GEL.

45. Hooker to Shaw, August 10, 1857, MBG Archives.

46. Engelmann to Shaw, August 11, 1857, MBG Archives.

47. Engelmann noted the marked contrast between Kew and "noisy Paris."

48. After being informed of Engelmann's planned visit, and aware of his expertise in the study of cacti, Hooker had insisted on giving Asa Gray a personal tour of the Kew cactus collection when he visited, hoping that Gray would communicate the extent of the Kew holdings to Engelmann in anticipation of his visit and subsequent study. As cited in Timberlake, *Engelmann: Scientist,* 109.

49. Shaw to Engelmann, October 18, 1856, GEL.

50. Shaw to Engelmann, September 15, 1857, GEL.

51. Engelmann to Gray, October 30, 1858, as cited in Timberlake, *Engelmann: Scientist,* 114; Engelmann to Gray, April 15, 1859, as cited in *MBGB* 30, no. 5 (1942): 103.

52. Engelmann to Gray, June 12, 1860, as cited in ibid., 107.

53. Engelmann to Shaw, November 1, 1860, as cited in ibid.

54. Loudon uses the terms "grand divisions" and "grand parts"; see his reference to Linnaean arrangement, *Encyclopedia of Gardening* (1850), 369.

55. The *Guide to the Garden,* MBG Archives, plant lists of 1856–60, two drawings, and early photographs are the few remaining pieces of evidence that illustrate what Shaw's original garden was like. Constant additions and improvement of the grounds over the first thirty-year period, and the fact that plant houses and sculpture were moved and reused, depict the evolution of the garden but make it difficult to pinpoint exact dates.

56. A "fruticetum" is defined by the *Oxford English Dictionary* (2d ed., 1989) as "a place full of shrubs and bushes," not restricted to fruit-bearing types. The dictionary cites Loudon's use of the term (*Encyclopedia of Gardening*, 2nd ed., p. 1059) as an example of its usage, "three grand parts . . . a circumference, displaying the arboretum, fruticetum, and ornamental flowers."

57. Sources differ on the exact size of the early garden. In his written "Reminiscences," Shaw indicates the garden as a whole to be 50–60 acres, while the official 1890 report describes it as being 44.7. The inconsistency may have to do with different estimates of the exact perimeter of the arboretum, which was contiguous with other land owned by Shaw.

58. Loudon invented the ridge-and-furrow roof and illustrated it in his *Encyclopedia of Gardening,* illustrations 610 and 182. Paxton was using it at Chatsworth by 1832 and at lesser known estates, such as Burton Closes, at Bakewell, Derbyshire (near Chatsworth), in 1846. Another example of this roof type that Shaw would have seen was at the Sheffield Botanic Garden.

59. See George Pring, "Henry Shaw's Arboretum," *MBGB* 52, no. 5 (1964): 1–7.

60. The garden supplied trees for Tower Grove Park and for planting along streets in the vicinity. Professor William Trelease, the director of the garden after Shaw's death, overlooked this function, stating that "for some reason [the arboretum] was planted with the trees in rows, as in a nursery." *Popular Science Monthly*, January 1903, 206.

61. For example, see the Utens lunettes of the Medici villas around Florence for plantings of this nature. A quincunx pattern is a linear pattern of fives organized within a given space (usually square).

62. See Loudon's suggestions in his *Encyclopedia*, 1012, and illustration 869.

63. Loudon, *Encyclopedia,* 639. Such a "prospect-tower" was, Loudon said, "a noble object to look at, and a gratifying and instructive position to look from."

64. Just as plant houses and sculpture were moved about the garden as needed, it is possible these covered seats were moved as well. Photographs suggest the fruticetum seat was later placed to the west of the (1868) glass conservatory, a move that would have made sense, the fruticetum area being less used after the construction of the large plant house that terminated the garden at its north end.

65. A similar decorative feel was evident on the rear of Shaw's villa prior to the improvements made after his death. Such embellishments were the first to go when tastes changed, because they were then perceived as too extravagant.

66. Loudon, *Encyclopedia,* 1010. Shaw's willingness to deviate from Loudon's advice to accommodate his personal taste is evident here: Loudon suggests this flower garden as "suitable to a castellated mansion; but would not suit a villa in the Italian style," which is what Shaw had.

67. John Claudius Loudon, *The Suburban Gardener, and Villa Companion* (London: Orme, Brown, Green and Longmans, 1838), 530.

68. "Great Work," an 1859 account that describes the early garden, in *MBGB* 18, no. 7 (1930): 121–22.

69. Engelmann to Gray, August 3, 1859, *MBGB* 30, no. 5 (1942): 105.

70. Reports of the case appeared in national publications such as the *New York Illustrated News*. A writer for the St. Louis publication *Reedy's Mirror* described Shaw as having "turned from the dreary monotony of spikes and mauls to the heavenly ecstasy of flowers" and Carstang as willowy and gorgeous, with "cheeks that caused roses to look up."

71. Thomas Meehan, ed., "The Botanic Garden, St. Louis, Mo.," *The Gardener's Monthly and Horticultural Advisor,* August 1868.

72. Shaw to Engelmann, January 13, 1858, GEL.

73. Shaw to Engelmann, September 15, 1857, and January 13, 1858, GEL.

74. St. Louis *Republic,* Sunday, June 9, 1895.

75. It was the sixth duke of Bedford who established the fine collection of exotic plants at Woburn prior to his death in 1839. George H. Pring, "Garden Maintenance," *MBGB* 52, no. 6 (1964): 8–12.

76. Dimmock, "Henry Shaw." Gurney "contributed very largely to make Garden and Park what they are now. Mr. Shaw's personal supervision of both was, however, never abandoned" (14).

77. Gurney said of his employer, "In twenty-three years I never heard him speak a harsh or irritable word." As cited in Faherty, *Henry Shaw,* 127.

78. James Gurney Jr. succeeded his father as Tower Grove Park superintendent from 1920 to 1943. His daughter, Bernice Gurney, has been the only woman to serve as park superintendent, from 1943 until her retirement in 1976.

79. More research needs to be conducted regarding this aspect of nineteenth-century American gardening, which differs markedly from English and European examples, because of our democratic system of government, economy, and American preferences in general. The role of the nineteenth-century gardener in society, wages, level of education, and so forth have yet to be dealt with in depth.

80. An anecdote in Jens Christian Bay, *In the House of Memories* (Cedar Rapids, Iowa: Torch Press, 1946), describes the discovery of these water lilies in British Guiana c. 1844 by Richard Schomburgk, and the duke of Bedford's acquisition of seeds. Presumably James Gurney was involved in the successful nurturing of the plants for the duke. Upon Queen Victoria's visit to the estate, he presented her with one of the blossoms. For Gurney's account of this event see St. Louis *Republic,* Sunday, June 9, 1895.

81. Henry Shaw letter dated January 24, 1869. Drawings and photographs suggest this reuse, and the 1869 letter confirms it. Moving even "permanent" buildings did not seem too daunting a task for Shaw. He left instructions that his town house was to be moved from downtown St. Louis to his country estate after his death. It was moved, brick by brick, in 1891.

82. Juno worked her way up the hierarchy of garden spaces and was "promoted" often. She moved about depending on where she was most needed. Between 1887 and 1913 she stood in front of Shaw's glass conservatory, then resided in the Italian parterre behind a second (newer) conservatory built in 1914. Today she stands just east of Shaw's house, in what has been designated the "Historic District," anchoring Victorian beds whose plants and design are based on the original sunken parterre. This garden splendidly re-creates what has been lost and treats visitors to a taste of the exuberance experienced by those who visited a century earlier.

83. Though written around 1880, its evolution had taken place over twenty years.

84. Earlier in the nineteenth century florists' flowers were not those grown for sale in a shop but decorative plants, such as Shaw's picotee carnations, grown for floral competitions. The most "perfect" specimens of these had a circular outline, clarity of form, good texture, and smooth rather than jagged edges. See Ruth Duthie,

Florists' Flowers and Societies (Princes Risborough, U.K.: Shire Publications, 1988), 5–31.

85. As cited in Faherty, *Henry Shaw,* 149.

86. M. M. Yeakle, *The City of Saint Louis of Today* (St. Louis: J. Osmund Yeakle and Co., 1889), 124.

87. As cited in *MBGB* 18, no. 7 (1930): 120.

88. The prominent position had much to do with funding created by Shaw's careful planning and ensured by his will. Upon Shaw's death, the institution's endowment grew, making the new director, Professor William Trelease, head of a "better endowed establishment than any other of its kind which ever existed." *The Gardener's Chronicle* 7, no. 158 (January 4, 1890): 19.

89. William Cullen Bryant, ed., *Picturesque America* (New York: Appleton, 1874), 324.

90. For contemporary accounts on visits to the garden, see "Open Sunday at Shaw's Garden," (St. Louis) *Republic,* September 6, 1897; "A Peep Into Shaw's Garden," *St. Louis Post-Dispatch*, August 28, 1891; and "Shaw's Garden Open Today," (St. Louis) *Globe,* September 5, 1892.

91. Jane Turner Censer, ed., *The Papers of Frederick Law Olmsted,* vol. 4, *Defending the Union* (Baltimore: Johns Hopkins University Press, 1986), 586.

Chapter 3

1. George Engelmann to Asa Gray, August 17, 1861.

2. The board was made up of five to seven commissioners. The original park commissioners were Mayor Thomas, Adolphus Meier, Judge William P. Ferguson, Charles Chouteau, and Shaw, whose position was to be filled by the director of the Missouri Botanical Garden after his death. This unique method of overseeing a public entity is still in place today.

3. A letter from the Massachusetts Horticultural Society, October 10, 1889, Box 48, series 4, Tower Grove Park Archives.

4. *Magazine of Horticulture* 11 (1845): 122–28. Hovey suggested these be financed privately by men of wealth.

5. Charles Sprague Sargent as cited in John Conron, *American Picturesque* (University Park: Pennsylvania State University Press, 2000), 181.

6. Almerin Hotchkiss, responsible for the landscape at Green-Wood, left the Brooklyn cemetery and went west to oversee Bellefontaine's development. He was in charge there for forty-six years.

7. Loudon, *On Laying Out, Planting, and Managing of Cemeteries and on the Improvement of Churchyards.* For more on the relationship of British and American cemeteries, see Andrew Clayden and Jan Woudstra, "Cemetery," in Candice A. Shoemaker, ed., *Encyclopedia of Gardens: History and Design* (Chicago: Fitzroy Dearborn, 2001), 249 ff.

8. The copper Willow Tree fountain surprised unsuspecting visitors who were drenched by water spurting from its branches.

9. Loudon, ed., "Some Account of the Arboretum lately commenced by His Grace the Duke of Devonshire, at Chatsworth, in Derbyshire" (as communicated by Joseph Paxton as Head Gardener and Forester of the estate), in Loudon, ed., *Gardener's Magazine* (August 1835): 385–95.

10. Paxton's original plan did not include areas for sports and group games, but spaces were identified as the need arose. A cricket ground was added at Birkenhead (and included in the Greensward plan of Central Park) and Shaw's plan cites "the children's playground & cricket ground." See Hazel Conway, "Sports and Playgrounds and the Problem of Park Design in the Nineteenth Century," *Journal of Garden History* 8, no. 1 (1988): 31–41, for a discussion on how spaces for active sports were (and were not) dealt with in park planning.

11. A similar plan was instigated by John Nash at Regent's Park, London, designed for the prince regent and opened in 1838, which incorporated villas and a park-like setting. In concept the Paxton plan is similar to that by Nash, the distinction being that Nash's villas appealed to (and would have been affordable only for) a much wealthier clientele than Paxton's, which were designed with smaller lots, for middle-class customers.

12. Shaw's plan is also strikingly similar to that of the Pittville Estate and Spa at Cheltenham, Gloucestershire, a place Shaw visited. See Steven Blake, *Pittville 1824–1860: A Scene of Gorgeous Magnificence* (Cheltenham, U.K.: Cheltenham Art Gallery & Museums, 1988).

13. Receipts indicate Shaw stayed at the Tontine Hotel in Sheffield and then at the Hen and Chicks Hotel in Birmingham on that trip. Derby is situated almost exactly between the two cities. Henry Shaw Business Papers, Hotel Receipts, 1840, MBG Archives.

14. Despite the shared origin and mission there are clear differences between the two parks. Derby Arboretum's eleven acres compared to Tower Grove Park's nearly three hundred acres makes size a primary difference. Loudon's plan does not include a carriage drive, only walking paths, which may have been dictated by size. At the arboretum, sinuous mounds were built up to create a sense of enclosure, and they contrast greatly with Tower Grove's relatively flat terrain. Loudon did include a few flower gardens near the perimeter, and vases for flowers at the junction of walks, because of Strutt's request that extant elements on the site (certain mature trees, an ivy-covered toolshed, and a flower garden) be incorporated into the plan. Loudon's statement that a greenhouse "would involve much more expense" is echoed by Shaw's observation that plant houses "would incur a large additional sum."

15. For a discussion of the role of financing in public parks and the problems of support for local authorities created by gifts of land by benefactors, see Hazel Conway, *People's Parks: The Design and Development of Victorian Parks in Britain* (Cambridge, U.K.: Cambridge University Press, 1991), 46.

16. The collection of trees as the basis for a public park did not excite everyone. See A. A. Tait, "The Return to Formality," in Elisabeth MacDougall, ed., *John Claudius Loudon and the Early Nineteenth Century in Britain* (Washington, D.C.: Dumbarton Oaks, 1980). "It was here that soulless appendage of the nineteenth-century garden, the arboretum, was born," 65.

17. Joseph Strutt in Loudon, *Derby Arboretum,* 83.

18. Shaw, *The Plan,* 7. Shaw goes on to note "the scientific or botanical names under the inspection of our learned fellow citizen Doct Geo Engelmann, as a guarantee of their correctness." Loudon includes a reference to his inspecting plants to ensure correct nomenclature, writing that "much of the usefulness of this Arboretum will depend on the nomenclature being correct," 81.

19. Christopher Hussey, *The Picturesque: Studies in a Point of View* (London: Putnam's Sons, 1927. Reprint, London: Cass, 1967), and Malcolm Andrews, *The Search for the Picturesque: Landscape Aesthetics and Tourism in Britain, 1760–1800* (Stanford, Calif.: Stanford University Press, 1989).

20. Hussey, *The Picturesque.* Also see Ann Bermingham, *Landscape and Ideology: The English Rustic Tradition 1740–1860* (Berkeley: University of California Press, 1986), and Stephen Daniels, *Fields of Vision: Landscape Imagery and National Identity in England and the United States* (Princeton, N.J.: Princeton University Press, 1993).

21. Edmund Burke's *An Enquiry into the Sublime and the Beautiful* (1757) broadened the ways art could be appreciated and expanded aesthetic perceptions by defining emotional counterparts to visual entities.

22. See Stephen Copley and Peter Garside, eds., *The Politics of the Picturesque: Literature, Landscape, and Aesthetics Since 1770* (New York: Cambridge University Press, 1994).

23. Andrew Ballantyne, *Aesthetics, Landscape, and Liberty: Richard Payne Knight and the Picturesque* (New York: Cambridge University Press, 1997).

24. John Conron, *American Picturesque* (University Park: Pennsylvania State University Press, 2000). Conron argues that the picturesque is the first American aesthetic (xvii). See his discussion of the complicated process of how the picturesque was appropriated in America.

25. For a discussion of how geology informed American landscape painting, see Rebecca Bedell, *The Anatomy of Nature* (Princeton, N.J.: Princeton University Press, 2001).

26. Conron, *American Picturesque.*

27. Shaw's journal and receipts document his tours around the Peak District, through the West Country, and in the Midlands. In 1840 he visited the countryside between Sheffield, Birmingham, and Leamington Spa; his 1842 tour included Devonshire and Liverpool; 1843 receipts indicate a visit to Liverpool and a stay at the Royal Hotel, Matlock. Documentation for 1851 includes a request for a guide and ponies to the waterfalls near Snowdon Peak, Wales. MBG Archives.

28. Shaw, "The Plan," 3–4.

29. Loudon, *Gardener's Magazine* 8 (December 1832).

30. John Claudius Loudon, ed., *The Landscape Gardening and Landscape Architecture of the Late Humphry Repton* (London: Whitehead, 1840), viii.

31. Loudon, *Encyclopedia,* 487.

32. Loudon, ed., *Repton's Landscape Gardening,* 215.

33. At Birkenhead Park, outside Liverpool, Joseph Paxton originally included bedding out only along the periphery. Chadwick, in *The Park and the Town,* writes that "it is unfortunate that the recent introduction of flower beds and rustic pergolas in the western half of the park entirely spoil the effect which Paxton had previously secured here," and "it is precisely this intrusion of small-scale flower beds and fussy, inappropriate detail which Repton, Nash, Loudon and Paxton warned against: it formed no part of their designs" (70). Loudon felt the common pleasure ground to be an insipid experience for the repeat visitor, suggesting the use of flowers alone to be a fatiguing ordeal, one that forced visitors to stoop down repeatedly in order to admire them closely. Loudon, *The Plan for Derby Arboretum,* 72. He does discuss the use of flowers for exhibition purposes during the winter season (77).

34. For antigardenesque commentary, see T. H. D. Turner, "Loudon's Stylistic Development," *Journal of Garden History* 2, no. 2 (1982): 175–88, and Tait, "The Return to Formality," in MacDougall, ed., *John Claudius Loudon.* For commentary relating to the gardenesque and the American Midwest, see Wilhelm Miller, *The Prairie Spirit in Landscape Gardening* (Amherst: University of Massachusetts Press, 2002).

35. Jellicoe, *Oxford Companion to Gardens,* 211.

36. Loudon, *Encyclopedia,* 487.

37. Shaw, "The Plan," 4.

38. "[T]he aesthetic element . . . contributes much to the education of the entire household in refinement, intellectual development, and moral sensibility," Catherine Beecher and Harriet Beecher Stowe, in *The American Woman's Home,* as cited in Conron, *American Picturesque,* 231.

39. David Schuyler, *Apostle of Taste: Andrew Jackson Downing 1815–1852* (Baltimore: Johns Hopkins University Press, 1996); Judith K. Major, *To Live in the New World* (Cambridge, Mass.: MIT Press, 1997); and George B. Tatum and Elisabeth B. MacDougall, eds., *Prophet With Honor: The Career of Andrew Jackson Downing 1815–1852* (Washington, D.C.: Dumbarton Oaks, 1987).

40. Olmsted understood the picturesque as a concept and considered Uvedale Price's definition of the term and his careful study of its application to be an important treatise pertaining to landscape ideology. See David Schuyler and Jane Turner Censer, eds., *The Years of Olmsted, Vaux and Co.,* vol. 6 (Baltimore: Johns Hopkins University Press, 1992), letter dated October 5, 1871, 470. Both Olmsted and Vaux appreciated Loudon's work and acknowledged it as an influence on their park projects. See Francis Kowsky, *Country, Park, & City: The Architecture and Life of Calvert Vaux* (New York: Oxford University Press, 1998).

41. Faherty, *Henry Shaw*, 193.

42. David MacAdam, *Tower Grove Park* (St. Louis: R. P. Studley and Co., 1883), 18. This publication recounts the park's origins, its physical layout, and aesthetic concerns based on Henry Shaw's "Plan of the Park and Reasons for Its Adoption," often elaborating on Shaw's comments, in descriptive prose.

43. Loudon, *Encyclopedia of Gardening,* 457–58.

44. MacAdam, *Tower Grove Park,* 19.

45. For discussion of the idea of middle landscape, see Leo Marx, *The Machine in the Garden: Technology and the Pastoral Ideal in America* (New York: Oxford University Press, 1964).

46. Shaw, Journal entry, January 24, 1869. MBG Archives.

47. The word "adoption" here implying "use," as the Oxford English Dictionary defines the verb "adopt," to "use as one's own."

48. The plan appears to have been a working document, based on notations made in the margins and its somewhat abrupt ending, suggesting the intention of adding commentary. Undated, it appears to have been written in the late 1860s or early 1870s, based on certain comments ("at present the trees are all small, and the beauty of the view is of necessity reserved for the future"), and it documents ideas that evolved over decades.

49. In 1827 John Claudius Loudon had begun a campaign to systematically plant thoroughfares and parks, not only for beauty, but to educate the public.

50. Shaw, "The Plan," 8. For comments on the Boulevard Law, see Sandweiss, *St. Louis: The Evolution of an American Urban Landscape*. It should be noted that Shaw not only suggested planting trees elsewhere in the city but that November 1873 park records contain a list of trees supplied to the city of St. Louis (and accepted by Superintendent of Parks, M. G. Kern) for planting at several parks including Benton Park, St. Louis Place, Laclede Park, and Hyde Park.

51. Shaw, "The Plan," 4.

52. That he was born in England only strengthened the importance of the reference.

53. The field of horticultural journalism began in the early nineteenth century. Practical advice, published on a weekly or monthly basis in various periodicals, addressed the concerns of professional gardeners but increasingly appealed to a popular audience that viewed horticulture as an avocation. J. C. Loudon's *Gardener's Magazine,* beginning publication in 1826, aimed to "disseminate new and improved information on all topics connected with horticulture, and to raise the intellect and character of those engaged in this art." Other British publications included Joseph Paxton's *Gardeners' Chronicle* (1841, "a weekly record of everything that bears upon Horticulture, or Garden Botany") and Jane Webb Loudon's *Ladies Magazine of Gardening* (1841), which specifically addressed women gardeners. In this country were A. J. Downing's *The Horticulturalist* (1846), *Meehan's Monthly,* and Charles Mason Hovey's *Magazine of Horticulture*.

54. Shaw's papers include a copy of the Central Park regulations (a small booklet listing the specific rules to be followed by visitors within the park), with words

added and struck from the text, which Shaw used as a template for Tower Grove Park's regulations. Shaw also made reference to Central Park and "Brooklyn Park" (presumably Prospect Park) in the Tower Grove Park second annual report (1871), citing cost of maintenance, improvements, and size as a comparison with his project, but he made no reference to the appearance or aesthetic characteristics of either. For the most recent discussion of Olmsted, Vaux, and their work see Charles A. Birnbaum and Robin Karson, eds., *Pioneers of American Landscape Design* (New York: McGraw-Hill, 2000). See also Roy Rosenzweig and Elizabeth Blackmar, *The Park and the People: A History of Central Park* (New York: Henry Holt, 1994).

55. It is generally agreed that Alphand's alterations of the Bois de Boulogne were based on the picturesque tradition established by the English in the second half of the eighteenth century. See Chadwick, *The Park and the Town,* regarding Alphand's plans: the relationship of "most of the parks of Paris of the time—to the parks of London was self-confessed and largely obvious," and "Alphand subscribes to many current English views on park and garden layout" (154).

56. Shaw, "The Plan," 6.

57. Loudon "ardently wished to make these objects, native and exotic trees—for centuries the objects of exclusive possession—accessible to all." Melanie Simo, *Loudon and the Landscape: From the Country Seat to Metropolis 1783–1843* (New Haven: Yale University Press, 1988), 165. See also Douglas Chambers, *The Planters of the English Landscape Garden: Botany, Trees and the Georgics* (New Haven: Yale University Press, 1993).

58. Tower Grove Park was listed on the National Register of Historic Places on March 17, 1972, and became a National Historic Landmark on December 20, 1989. At that time, the only other parks with this distinction were Central Park, Boston Public Garden, and Boston Common. For specific information on each park structure, see the Historic American Buildings Survey for Tower Grove Park, 1974–75 (with revisions and additions made in 1983), Tower Grove Park (TGP) Archives, which is located at the park office in the restored 1885 palm house, now known as the Piper Plant House.

59. Shaw recorded that the summerhouse on the Children's Playground was planted with honeysuckle and trumpet vines, and the 1871 report lists the two sequentially. He also indicated that the plantings for the labyrinth were of hemlock and Norway spruce, which are listed together at the beginning of the inventory.

60. At the center of the labyrinth, a hexagonal-towered pavilion (similar to one at Shaw's garden) overlooked the maze of hedges. Both labyrinth and pavilion were razed in 1908, victims of budget restraints and changing taste.

61. Recently restored by major fundraising efforts, the palm houses are now exceptional examples of adaptive reuse, one housing the park office and archives, the other used for special social events, much in keeping with Shaw's original intentions.

62. Barnett became an important architect in the Midwest and was a charter mem-

ber of the American Institute of Architects. His St. Louis commissions included the Lindell Hotel, the church of St. Vincent de Paul, and the Equitable Building, in addition to projects for Shaw. Barnett's son, Thomas P. Barnett, also an architect, was involved with work for the 1904 World's Fair in St. Louis and the Cathedral of St. Louis (1914).

63. For the rich and complicated effect of "Orientalist" design as it relates to the nineteenth-century American audience see Holly Edwards, ed., *Noble Dreams, Wicked Pleasures: Orientalism in America, 1870–1930* (Princeton, N.J.: Princeton University Press and Sterling and Francine Clark Art Institute, 2000).

64. M. M. Yeakle, *The City of Saint Louis of Today* (St. Louis: J. Osmund Yeakle and Co., 1889), 124.

65. MacAdam, *Tower Grove Park,* 22.

66. Annual Report for Tower Grove Park, January 1, 1879. TGP Archives.

Chapter 4

1. Dupree, *Asa Gray,* 402–3.

2. Gray to J. D. Hooker, June 9, 1884, as cited in *MBGB* 30, no. 5 (1942). "I went on to St. Louis. Mr. Shaw took me into his counsel and . . . I see there is a grand opportunity coming, and I think that none of the provisions he has made will hinder the right development of the Mississippian Kew, which will hardly be Kew in a corner" (109).

3. Shaw to Gray, March 9, 1887. MBG Archives.

4. Shaw left friends and associates personal items; for example, he gave George Barnett a clock, a bottle of sherry, and an oil painting. Family (including his housekeeper Rebecca Edom) received money and property (from lots to entire city blocks). Nine institutions were awarded $1,000 each, and garden and park employees with five years seniority received $75.00 each.

5. Trelease (1857–1945) came to the garden in 1885, one year after he earned his Ph.D. from Harvard under William Farlow. His undergraduate degree was from Cornell University; experience before coming to Missouri included fieldwork and teaching at the University of Wisconsin, Madison, as a lecturer at Johns Hopkins, and directing the botanical program at Harvard.

6. To advocate for the park, and help raise public awareness of its value and cultural contribution to the city, David MacAdam's descriptive narrative, with illustrations, *Tower Grove Park,* was published in 1883.

7. *St. Louis Republic,* June 26, 1904.

8. *Tower Grove Park Annual Report,* 1896, 10.

9. *Tower Grove Park Annual Report,* 1899, 8. The need for these additions to be "sanctioned" suggests deliberate action by the board in the memory, and according to the will, of Henry Shaw. Alteration was done cautiously the first years af-

ter Shaw's death; in the 1891 annual report, for example, the board insisted on maintaining the gardenesque character of the park despite its expense.

10. Brent Elliott, *Victorian Gardens,* 134–35.

11. Edgar Anderson, "Victoria Water Lilies," *MBGB* 53, no. 5 (1965): 1–18.

12. Trelease, *Popular Science Monthly*, January 1903. Trelease described the fruticetum as closed to the ordinary visitor due to the nature of (or lack of) its present use, 206.

13. "St. Louis Botanic Garden," *The Gardeners' Chronicle* 7, no. 158 (1890): 19.

14. "Garden Scholarships," *The Gardeners' Chronicle* 7, no. 159 (1890): 49.

15. Stylistically, the Casino was an eclectic combination of mansard roof, gingerbread trim, and dormers, which expressed the architectural interests of the third quarter of the century and mirrored many of the pavilions and decorative elements in the garden. As part of the garden improvements, the board voted to have it torn down in May 1896.

16. When Trelease, as new director of the garden, moved into Shaw's villa in 1890, a new east wing was added to the house, as were improved plumbing and heating. Similar updates were made to conservatories and workshops.

17. Some trustees and related parties believed that the leasing of garden land for residential purposes was against Shaw's will. An August 17, 1896, Missouri Supreme Court decree empowered the garden trustees to sell this real estate, allowing funds to be generated and used by the garden.

18. A shortened version of this report was published in the Eighth Annual Report of the Director (1897): 37–46. Trelease also forecasts future problems, for example, the "smoke and soot" of the city as a hindrance to propagating the orchids the garden was becoming known for.

19. Much of this unimproved land to the west of the garden was sold off in 1923 and subsequently developed into residential property. The income was used to purchase 2,400 acres on the Meramec River at Gray Summit, Missouri, thirty-five miles southwest of St. Louis. This land, called the Shaw Arboretum, had multiple uses, one of them to house the garden's increasingly valuable orchid collection, which was threatened by city air so polluted that it deposited a layer of soot onto the plant's leaves.

20. Director Charles Sprague Sargent and Frederick Law Olmsted used the Bentham and Hooker organization at the Arnold Arboretum in the 1870s. See Stephen S. Sponberg, "The Bentham and Hooker Planting Sequence in the Arnold Arboretum," *Arnoldia* 49, no. 1 (1989).

21. In a letter dated February 16, 1912, to his mentor William Farlow, Trelease makes this implication, although he says he would prefer "more garden but no less science." Farlow Library and Herbarium, Harvard University, Farlow Papers. As cited in Emanuel Rudolph, "One Hundred Years of the Missouri Botanical Garden," *Annals of the Missouri Botanical Garden* 78, no. 1 (1991).

22. Evidence of disagreement about the garden additions and alterations, including the comment "I sent this for your inspection, expecting you will consider it fit for

the wastebasket," exists in the letter to Trelease from Leonard Matthews, Board of Trustees, which accompanies the Olmsted preliminary report of May 1897.

23. St. Louis *Post-Dispatch*, December 18, 1903.

24. Trelease to Farlow, February 16, 1912.

25. Trelease may have discussed the basis of this plan with Frederick Law Olmsted when he visited St. Louis in 1892 (Olmsted had taken a break from work on the grounds of the Columbian Exposition, to be held in Chicago in 1893).

26. Although it was Frederick Law Olmsted Sr. who first consulted on the garden project it was probably John Charles Olmsted who attended the board meeting on April 22, 1896, since Olmsted Sr.'s health would have prohibited him from doing so.

27. Eighth Annual Report of the Director, 37.

28. During this period the Olmsted firm was working to create a plan that would please both the trustees and Trelease, but there were changes within the firm that certainly affected its performance, such as the official retirement of the senior Olmsted and the untimely death of partner Charles Eliot.

29. "The improvements carried out by the founder [should] be preserved and embodied in the future improvements, not merely from regard for his personality or on account of the possible economy . . . but because there is a quaintness and a pleasant appeal to the sympathies in preserving for their historical interest (even where artistic merit is somewhat lacking) the worthy works of past generations." *Formal Report Accompanying Preliminary Plans,* June 1897, 4.

30. John Charles Olmsted to William Trelease, March 5, 1898. MBG Archives.

31. Marnock, and other landscape gardeners including Loudon, understood that the choice of method or aesthetic was dependent on the circumstances, and that one could embrace a variety of approaches. Our present understanding of these professionals tends to align them with one particular aesthetic, but it appears that many of them applied several aesthetics as determined by the requirements of the job at hand.

32. Frederick Law Olmsted to William Hooker, as cited in David Schuyler and Jane Turner Censer, eds., *The Years of Olmsted, Vaux & Company, 1865–1874,* vol. 6 of *The Papers of Frederick Law Olmsted* (Baltimore: Johns Hopkins University Press, 1992), 6. He implied that these methods were "suitable to the housefurnishing & millinery trades," 424.

33. The final plan of 1905 incorporated a greater interest in decorative gardening than the preliminary plan of May 6, 1897, submitted by "FL and JC Olmsted," with its emphasis on the science of botany.

34. Some aspects of the Olmsted plan were strikingly similar to the methods they criticized. For example, their formal gardens were to be planted in symmetrical patterns with the plants being changed once or twice per year, resulting in a similar look and labor-intensive maintenance as Victorian precursors such as carpet bedding, and their "singular" planting of trees is basically the same approach as Loudon's specimen plantings.

35. To make way for this new conservatory, one of the last vestiges of Shaw's original garden, the stone wall that had delineated the western edge of the main garden proper and had provided shelter for growing figs, was removed, physically and visually opening up the garden by increasing its size and expanding the view toward the west.

36. A total of 95 plans and drawings and 741 sheets of plant lists exist in the Olmsted archives for the Job #81, the Missouri Botanical Garden.

37. Minutes of the December 14, 1904, meeting of the board of trustees of the Missouri Botanical Garden.

38. Pring had succeeded George Edward McClure, who returned to work for his family's landscape business in Buffalo, and who later specialized in the planning of cemeteries. Pring remained on staff until 1962, and later consulted for Longwood Gardens in Kennet Square, Pennsylvania.

39. See Faherty, *Henry Shaw,* 197. In the early years of the program, of the eight doctoral candidates and six master's candidates to receive degrees, four were women. Isabel Mulford was the first woman to receive a doctorate from the Shaw School of Botany in 1895.

40. By this time students (and probably their instructors) were referring to the elaborate botanical sequence of the herbaceous grounds as the "weed patch," as cited in George H. Pring, "Garden Maintenance," *MBGB* 52, no. 6 (1964): 8–12.

41. *MBGB* 1, no. 5 (1913): 69.

42. Ibid., 65.

Index

Note: Page numbers in *italics* indicate photographs or illustrations. Plant names are those used by Henry Shaw.

French settlers, in St. Louis, 198 n.13
fritillaria, crown imperial, 54
fruit trees, 37
fruticetum, MBG
    closure of, 210 n.12
    covered seat, *85, 201* n.64
    definition, 200 n.56
    in 1889 drawing, *71, 165*
    entrance to, 87
    as grand division, 71, 97
    pavilion, *74*
    purpose of, 63, 70
    reduced use of, 95
    southern boundary of, 72
    trenching in, *64*
    visual pattern of, 81–82
fuchsia, 41
furnishings, in HS's town house, 34
fur trade, HS and, 24

games, areas for, 204 n.10
garden accessories, 52
garden beds
    bedding out, 86, 206 n.33
    carpet bedding, 123, 175, 211 n.34
    changeable, *68, 79, 79*
    organization methods, 80–81, *82,*
        83–84, *83, 84*
    in Tower Grove Park, *162*
    See also flower beds
garden botany, 5, 43, 98, 100
    See also botany
Garden Bulletin, 183, 186
garden cemeteries, 107–8
garden design
    color theory in, 44, 80, 81, 196 n.31
    Loudon on, 86, 200 n.54
    twentieth-century, 39
    See also gardening; garden organiza-
        tion methods; landscape gardening
gardeners
    gentleman, role of, 6
    nineteenth-century, role of, 202 n.79

professional, 80, 207 n.53
    responsibilities of, 115
    scholarships for training of, 168–69
    at Tower Grove Park, 148
    See also Gurney, James
Gardener's Chronicle, 100, 207 n.53
Gardener's Magazine, 51, 65, *81,* 110–11,
    207 n.53
Gardener's Monthly, 78, 100, 207 n.53
gardenesque, the
    art *vs.* nature, 120
    criticisms of, 123
    decline of, 124
    description of, 52–53
    individual perfection and, 120–21
    Loudon on, 109
    as nineteenth-century aesthetic, 126
    preservation of, at MBG, 209 n.7
    at Sheffield Botanic Garden, 52, 175
    specimen plantings and, 97, 120, *121,*
        122, *122*
    See also ornamental elements
garden forms, 72, 83–84
gardening
    art of, as HS priority, 69
    as botany-related hobby, 19, 42
    HS's enthusiasm for, 27
    instruments of, 42, 53
    as profession, 80, 202 n.79, 207 n.53
        (*See also* gardeners)
    at Tower Grove (estate), 41
Gardening for Pleasure (Henderson),
    39
garden journals, 42–44, 48
    See also account books
garden organization methods
    Bentham and Hooker method, 210
        n.20
    botanical classification, 80
    with gardenesque approach, 52
    grand divisions, 71, 110–11
    William Hooker on, 64–65
    HS's plans for, 66, 140